THE WAY OF SPIRITUAL DISCERNMENT

SACRED
COMPASS

J. BRENT BILL

Foreword by
RICHARD J. FOSTER

PARACLETE PRESS
Brewster, Massachusetts

DEDICATION

*To the Friends in Fellowship worship group
who walked with me and guided me as I wrote this book.*

Sacred Compass: The Way of Spiritual Discernment

2008 First Printing

Copyright © 2008 by J. Brent Bill

ISBN: 978-1-55725-559-4

Copyright notices for the Bible versions used in this edition are listed on the "Permissions" pages at the end of the book.

Author's Note: The names of people in some of the stories have been changed to protect their anonymity. The stories are factual and occurred as written. None of the people are composite characters.

Library of Congress Cataloging-in-Publication Data
Bill, J. Brent, 1951-
  Sacred compass : the way of spiritual discernment / J. Brent Bill.
      p. cm.
  Includes bibliographical references.
  ISBN-13: 978-1-55725-559-4
  1. Discernment (Christian theology) 2. Spirituality. I. Title.
  BV4509.5.B543 2008
  248.4—dc22
                                        2008001688

10 9 8 7 6 5 4 3 2 1

Published by Paraclete Press
Brewster, Massachusetts
www.paracletepress.com

Printed in the United States of America

CONTENTS

FOREWORD

I DO A GOOD DEAL OF HIKING: Leisure hiking. Trail hiking. Off-trail hiking. Wilderness hiking. Overnight hiking. Extended backpack hiking. And more. One piece of equipment that is always good to have along is a compass. Especially when I am "bushwhacking" off-trail in the high country of the Colorado Rockies.

I must admit to you that I have not graduated to a G.P.S. I resist it for some reason. Yes, I know, the technology of the G.P.S. makes it a far more accurate instrument. Still, I hold back. Perhaps it's that when I'm in the wilderness I want to be as far away from high-tech gadgetry as possible. I will even take off my watch and leave it at home.

But a compass is different somehow. A compass is an old friend. Maybe it is because the compass connects me, if only in a small way, to centuries of travelers of all kinds. Then, too, a compass guides me . . . but not perfectly. For one thing, I am always having to make the adjustments between magnetic north and true north. Also, a compass does not give me the details of a G.P.S. There are still lots of unknowns and plenty of decisions to make. I rather like that. I like the mystery. I like the unexpectedness. I like the adventure.

All of that to say that I think the metaphor of a compass is a good one when we are considering our life's journey in relation to God. With skillful use of this metaphor, Brent Bill has written one of the finest books on discernment and Divine guidance that I have seen in a very long time.

And that is saying something. In general, I do not care for the many modern books out in the marketplace on "Divine guidance." I wish I didn't have to say it, but these books almost always degenerate into simplistic, rigid systems for discerning the will of God. Thankfully, *Sacred Compass* stands apart from these easy solutions to life's perplexities. Its openness and flexibility is true to the realities of the frequent twists and turns of everyday life.

Brent Bill is a Quaker, and he warmly embraces this tradition. But never in a sectarian way. Most of the great spiritual insights are "loanable," and so when Bill draws from his Quaker heritage he is doing so in the spirit of the catholicity of sharing. This is true even when he utilizes special Quaker phrases: "as way opens," "let your life speak," "never run ahead of your leading," and more. He unpacks this Quaker language in such a warm and loving way that regardless of our denominational tradition we all are drawn into the reality of which the language speaks. In addition, it is clear that Bill is also engaging with a whole host of Christian traditions and showing that they all share the composite likeness of godliness.

There are many things I like about *Sacred Compass*. Let me mention four.

First, in his writing somehow Brent Bill is able to create "space" for us to become quiet and listen to God. The writing submerges us into prayer and allows space for the Divine/human dialogue, Spirit to spirit. It is quite amazing really. Maybe it's the author's openness and ease with us as readers. Perhaps it's the naturalness and grace that gives us permission to let go of our frantic ways. Maybe it's the freedom from strict categories of expectation and performance. For example, in a section on "Seasons of Discernment" Bill teaches about "sensing" and "waiting" and "acting." In the teaching he reminds us that we do not, "slavishly move from Sensing to Waiting to Acting, with each having clearly defined beginnings and endings. Instead, Waiting can lead back to Sensing or forward to Action. Likewise, Action can lead back to Sensing or Waiting. Often, the three are a synthesis of each other—a blend of Sensing and Waiting while Acting, for example. They flow one to another and back around." It is this openness and flexibility that calms my frenzied spirit. It quiets me, settles me, thickens me.

Second, *Sacred Compass* bravely engages the harshness and dissonance we experience in life that often punches us hard in the gut. At times even threatening to deliver a knock-out blow. (And, dear reader, if you have not yet experienced these tough realities, believe me, you will.) My two favorite chapters are "West of Eden: What if the Way Takes us to Unexpected Places?" and "The Dark Path; What if You Lose Your Way?"

"West of Eden" helps us understand that Divine guidance can, very frankly, lead to things we would never imagine or want when we started out: our own death, for example. "The

Dark Path" reminds us that God is still with us when we have walked down foreign paths and gone other ways. Listen: "In the New Testament the word *lost* means simply that—'lost.' It doesn't mean being doomed or damned for all eternity. It means that whatever is lost is in the wrong place; it's not where it should be. This is true in all of Jesus' parables (such as the one about the lost coin) and about people, too. Things and people are lost when they are not in the right place."

Third, *Sacred Compass* is eminently practical. I don't mean "practical" in the sense of giving exercises or tasks to do. It does do that to some extent, but that is not what I am referring to. No, I mean that the whole of the book is practical. It's the ease in approaching the subject matter. It's the anecdotal stories. It's the small, seemingly off-handed comments that startle us into thinking in new directions. It's all that, and more.

And finally, *Sacred Compass* is filled with such encouragement. There is no grit-our-teeth earnestness here. Divine guidance is ultimately life-giving and joy-filled. In reality the "sacred compass" is simply the Holy Spirit leading us to the face of a loving God. It is Jesus, the inner Teacher, showing us how to live fully, freely. Always there is a clear expectation that this life is genuinely possible. At one point Brent Bill says that we are discovering "a fresh and deeper way of living a God-directed life— a life that eschews simple spiritual solutions and invites us into the deepest, most soulful parts of our being." And so we are.

Richard J. Foster

THE HOLY DISCOVERY

A COMPASS, no matter what direction we turn, always points us to the north pole—a destination most of us (unless we're named Amundsen, Byrd, Peary, or Henson) will never reach in this lifetime. In that way, a compass makes a good metaphor for our spiritual lives and the work of discerning God's will for us.

Many times I wish God spoke as clearly and as obviously as Mapquest or Google Maps or a GPS. But God doesn't. Maybe that's because we don't navigate the life of faith via anything remotely resembling a GPS. Instead, the divine compass points us to our spiritual true north—the mind and love of God. Our sacred compass operates in our souls and calls us to life with God—life abundant and adventurous, even when we wish living was less of an adventure. The sacred compass leads us on a life of pilgrimage—a hike to wholeness and holiness.

In pointing us always to God, the compass helps us with our soul's deepest question, *What am I supposed to do with my life?* The question of how to live our lives especially presses on those of us who sense we are not merely humans trying to be spiritual, but are deeply spiritual beings endeavoring to live as fully human.

Every day begins with that "what" question. We wake up each morning with a cavalcade of choices before us—beginning with whether or not to get up. Things get more complicated from there. The very act of making a choice—any choice—shows us that our lives are more than our own. We belong to ourselves, but we also belong to others—our family, our neighbors, our pets, our coworkers. Most of all, we belong to God.

When I was in college, I encountered a group handing out little buff-colored booklets titled "The Four Spiritual Laws." The first spiritual law was, "God loves you and has a wonderful plan for your life." The idea that God has a plan for us is not a novel concept. The Bible and the whole of Christian history are full of examples of people seeking to determine God's will. In order to find God's will, women and men of faith cast lots, set out fleeces, prayed, fasted, learned to listen to donkeys, went on retreats, climbed up cacti, and more. These days, bookstores are crammed full of titles about learning God's will. Amazon.com alone offers more 38,000 books on the subject. While some of those books offer you five easy steps for discerning God's direction for you, this book is not one of them. Uncovering God's direction for us is not the five-easy-steps kind of simple.

Discovering spiritual direction is simple—but in an amazingly countercultural and counterintuitive way. It is about heeding the Holy Spirit. Learning to follow the divine compass means stopping and paying attention instead of looking for a magical map with the shortest route highlighted in yellow. Learning what God wants of us means letting the Holy Spirit guide us into the deep places of our souls. We learn to look for God in those deep places and in all the places our lives take us.

When we travel through life attentive to the sacred compass, we find that God's direction changes us. We discover that spiritual discernment is about sensing the presence and call of God, and not just about making decisions. The process of following the sacred compass awakens us to a life of constant renewal of our hearts, minds, wills, and souls.

This renewal moves us deep into personal spiritual transformation. And as we change, we also change the lives of the people around us and, ultimately, the world. Such transformation is not accomplished by following a pre-published route mapped out in *The God's Will Guidebook*. Rather, true transformation happens when we let the map (and any idea of a map) flutter from our tight grasp and instead begin to use the sacred compass that God provides—the compass of the Holy Spirit's work within us.

THE SACRED COMPASS SHOWS US GOD'S DIRECTION

That inner compass tells us that we can know God's direction for us. I picked the seminary I attended partly because of its motto—"We hold that Christ's will can be known and obeyed." I found the thought that I could know God's will called to my heart, and I don't think my heart is the only one that hears that call. When I surveyed some of my friends and readers, I found that almost 90 percent of them said that there was a time in their lives when they knew what God wanted them to do. Some of their experiences appear in this book. Their experiences of God's direction were as varied as the people I surveyed. While their God-encounters were unique, there were some similarities. Each of them said:

- they found it daunting to say that God led them
- their experience of divine direction was unmistakable
- their experience pointed them to God
- they were led to act

Writer Amy Frykholm's experience illustrates these aspects of God-encounter:

I'm very hesitant to say that "God wanted me to do something," and yet I have experienced times of extraordinary clarity when not only the direction that I should take seemed clear, but the workings of something beyond myself, the softening up of my whole self in order to accept a previously unacceptable direction, took place.

The most obvious example is a period when, after six years of graduate school, I abandoned the path clearly laid out for me toward an academic job and an academic life. Instead, after a long period of discernment that included long conversations and long silences, a lot of tears, a lot of giving up of ego, it became clear to me that another, less logical path, was the better one.

One of my guides during this time was the Sufi poet Hafez, and especially his poem, "Some fill with each good rain," and the lines: "There are different wells within your heart. Some fill with each good rain, Others are far too deep for that. In one well You have just a few precious cups of water, That 'love' is literally something of yourself, It can grow as slow as a diamond If it is lost."

The path that I was on seemed determined to deplete those few cups of water, and I knew, with some deep part of myself, that I would need to find another path if I wanted to be renewed.

THE SACRED COMPASS LEADS US TO HOLY DISCOVERY

Following our sacred compass leads us to a place where we learn from God in the daily and in the lifelong. This place is one of seeking and sensing God. It is a place of divine direction and spiritual opportunity. Learning to follow the sacred compass means living in a constant state of discernment and obedience to God.

The divine compass asks us to travel by faith and put to use the various maps we've been given—maps such as the Bible, prayer, spiritual friends, and other faith practices. Our compass takes us to a fresh and deeper way of living a God-directed life—a life that eschews simple spiritual solutions and invites us into the deepest, most soulful parts of our being.

Keeping our soul's eyes on the sacred compass leads us to the holy discovery that we can move through life with purpose and promise, even in those times when we may not sense with certainty what that purpose and promise are.

THE SACRED COMPASS COMPLEMENTS OUR UNIQUENESS

The sacred compass also shows us that the path of discernment is unique to each person. None of us follows the exact same paths as any other person. None of us has the exact same talents—or failings—as any other person. And God does not use us in the exact same way as any other person. There was only one Moses raised in Pharaoh's court, one Mary the mother of Jesus, one Martin Luther, one Julian of Norwich, and one you.

The sacred compass leads each of us to the life only we can live. Our compass calls us to use the gifts only we can give. In a grace-filled way, our compass invites us into a life of continuous experiences of God and of spiritual transformation. As we move toward divine guidance, we joyfully behold the face of a loving God gazing back at us.

ONE

AS WAY OPENS

Moving from Tourists to Pilgrims

WILL YOU BE COMING FOR DINNER TOMORROW?" one might ask. "I will, if way opens," a Quaker is likely to respond. Quakers, also known as Friends, have been known to drop "as way opens" into conversation as easily as other folks do "Hello" or "How're you doing?" It's almost become a cliché.

Yet, in spite of its colloquial use, we most often hear that phrase during deep discussions around important decisions. This saying speaks to the belief that God's revelation, even in daily life, continues for all who follow their sacred compass. God works within and around us, leading, guiding, and opening the way, sometimes when we least expect or feel it. The idea of being led and guided implies movement. If we're being led or guided then we must be being led or guided *somewhere*. The sacred compass shows us that we are on a pilgrimage to our spiritual true north—God.

As way opens implies a deep way of developing our spiritual insight, making major decisions, and planning. It is the condensed version of a longer phrase: "to proceed as way opens." There's that movement again—but it is movement with a cautionary note. Proceed, yes, but *only* as way opens.

Counter to our lives of action, the sacred compass tells us to take time to wait for God's guidance before moving ahead. Part of following way opening is learning to be less hasty—to take time to let the direction needle stop wobbling and point its way to God.

AS WAY OPENS IS A PILGRIMAGE

Way opening teaches us that the compass is about more than decision making. While we use its principles and tools to help make major life decisions—careers, life partners—and minor ones, a primary teaching of way opening is to base our movement on God's timing. Decisions big and small are portions of our life of pilgrimage, but they are not the destination. Life with God is the destination.

Whom we marry or don't, where we live or won't, certainly factor into our life's path. They influence its direction, but our journey continues no matter what decisions we make. That's why we need to learn to see God at work within and around us. When we behold God present with us, we find that our lives are lives of pilgrimage and not of static spiritual sitting.

PILGRIMS LEARN FROM OTHER PILGRIMS

Growing up, my religious training was steeped in the Bible. Of particular interest to me, as a kid, were the stories of children in the Bible. One of my favorites was the story of Samuel. He was a boy in a time when (as the King James Version puts it) "the word of the LORD was precious in those days; there was no open vision." Precious and open himself, Samuel heard God's voice, obeyed it, and came to be known as "a prophet of the Lord."

The idea that God could speak to a kid was pretty heady. Samuel's story taught us to listen to God and for God. Mrs. Clark, our Sunday school teacher, assured us that if we did listen, and if we heard God's voice and obeyed it, we would also be known for opening the vision of God and making God's word precious.

The Bible is filled with examples of people—young and not-so-young—who sought God's will. The early disciples looked for direction in replacing Judas. Joshua asked God about apportioning the land of Canaan to the people of Israel. Jesus, too, was an example of seeking God's will: while praying in the Garden prior to his passion, he sought confirmation of God's path for him: "And [Jesus] withdrew from them about a stone's throw, and knelt down and prayed, 'Father, if thou art willing, remove this cup from me; nevertheless not my will, but thine, be done.'" Jesus' path led to the cross, the grave, and ultimately, resurrection. For Jesus, the way opened into our forgiveness and our healing.

Christian church history is also replete with stories of women and men in quest of God's direction for their lives. These range from the desert fathers to Thomas à Kempis to Mother Teresa to the person who sits next to me in the pew each Sunday morning.

One of my favorite stories is that of St. Ignatius. Born in Spain in the early fifteenth century, the young Ignatius was no model of sainthood. Ignatius was pompous and obsessed with desire to win glory on the battlefield. Rejecting his father's wish for him to become a priest, Ignatius went on military adventures. During one battle, a cannon ball shattered his leg. While recovering in Loyola, he asked for books about romance and chivalry. Instead, he received books on the love of Christ and the lives of the saints. While reading, he discovered that his old dreams of romance and adventure left him unsettled and unhappy. The saints, in contrast, seemed serene even in horrible circumstances. With a shift of spirit, he felt called to a higher life of devotion to God and later wrote *Spiritual Exercises*. Now considered a spiritual classic, his book uses a four-week, systematic review of our personal spiritual lives to train the soul. They are considered a pilates for piety.

Ignatius's idea of "soul conditioning" or "spiritual sit-ups" was not original. St. Paul hinted at that idea 1,400 years earlier, when he wrote to Timothy, "train yourself to be godly. For physical training is of some value, but godliness has value for all things." With this training in mind, Ignatius took Paul's concept and turned it into a set of spiritual exercises that are still used to great effect today.

Recently, pastor and author Rick Warren has generated a new form of contemporary spiritual exercise around the themes of the purpose-driven life and forty days of purpose—all based on the tenet that a "healthy, balanced church helps develop changed lives—people who are driven by the five biblical purposes that God designed for every human life." According to Warren, the five purposes for our lives are worship, fellowship, discipleship, ministry, and missions. Millions of copies of his book *The Purpose-Driven Life* have been sold and thousands of churches have participated in a forty days of purpose campaign.

Men and women who find them helpful to their spiritual walk eagerly read books by Ignatius, Warren, and other spiritual explorers. We want to learn from others who have trod the pilgrim path. Their words enlighten, embolden, and beckon us onward. We often feel like we're on our journey alone. Writings of fellow pilgrims remind us that, while our way is unique to us, there are many, ancient and modern, who have traveled with us. I've traveled with Ignatius, Thomas Kelly, Anne Lamott, and a host of others. How about you? Who would make your list of fellow pilgrims? Whose writing do you read for companionship on the way?

PILGRIMS ARE LED BY THE HOLY SPIRIT

The concept of as way opens takes a different tack from either Ignatius or Warren. Instead of focusing on four-week spiritual exercises or forty-day programs, as way opens points us to the constant presence of the Holy Spirit in our lives. The Holy Spirit is our sacred compass; its role is to show us our way. Jesus said:

> If you love me, you will keep my commandments. And I will pray the Father, and he will give you another Counselor, to be with you for ever, even the Spirit of truth, whom the world cannot receive, because it neither sees him nor knows him; you know him, for he dwells with you, and will be in you.

This Gospel passage reminds us that God is with us on our pilgrimage—the indwelling Paraclete (a Greek word that is sometimes translated as "counselor") accompanies us. God gives us the Paraclete to guide us into God's truth. The Holy Spirit fulfills Christ's promise that God will be with us forever as it works in our souls, teaching and guiding us. As way opens is about learning to pay attention to this Inner Teacher, our sacred compass. When we do so, we see God's direction for our questions big and small, immediate and lifelong. We sense, through the work of the Paraclete, that God is always present with us, guiding and directing our lives. We witness the work of our personal sacred compass.

The early Friends believed that the Inner Teacher spoke with a quiet voice heard in the soul, so they worshiped in silence. They sought souls still enough to hear the God who speaks in sacred silence. They weren't the first to hear God's voice in soulful stillness. After God directed the prophet Elijah to go stand on a mountain, he discovered that God was not in the earthquake, wind, or fire, but in the sound of "sheer silence":

> "Go out and stand on the mountain before the LORD, for the LORD is about to pass by." Now there was a great wind, so strong that it was splitting mountains and breaking rocks in pieces before the LORD, but the LORD was not in the wind; and after the wind an earthquake, but the LORD was not in the earthquake; and after the earthquake a fire, but the LORD was not in the fire; and after the fire a sound of sheer silence. When Elijah heard it, he wrapped his face in his mantle and went out and stood at the entrance of the cave.

God's voice is at times so deep and so holy that it may appear to be nothing but silence—unless, like Elijah, we pay heartfelt attention. Can you think of a time when you heard God in the stillness of your soul? How did you get to that place of quietness and listening? When we quiet our soul's busy-ness, we hear the voice of the Inner Teacher showing us the way opening.

PILGRIMS CAN TAKE MANY PATHS

I grew up evangelical Quaker. We subscribed to the belief that "God loves you and has a wonderful plan for your life." As such, we spent a lot of time, especially as teenagers, trying to determine what this plan was, especially about things such as where to go to college, whom to marry, and what career to go into.

Some of these decisions were easy—our church had already discerned some of God's direction for our lives. In our case, the plan did not include smoking cigarettes, drinking alcohol, cursing, or dancing. If we went to college, we'd go to one of our church-affiliated schools. There were jobs we should take and others we couldn't. Bartending was out of the question. Many careers had carefully delineated gender roles. Young men could be pastors; young women could be pastor's wives. When we got married, we'd marry someone from our brand of Christianity, preferably someone from our local church. All of these guidelines were set up so that we could faithfully keep the first spiritual law and follow that wonderful plan God had for our lives.

And therein lies the rub—"*a* wonderful plan for your life." A. One plan. Notice I didn't say wonderful *plans* for your life.

The implication was that God had just one plan, which also implied that you'd best spend a lot of time making sure you knew what that plan was so you didn't mess it up.

As I grew older, questions arose. This idea of a plan also implied that there was a sort of map for our lives. Such a map would have clear directions—just the way a road map showed the way to get from Pingree to Lake Williams, North Dakota, a thirty-five-mile straight shot on North Dakota State Road 36.

My life was far from a thirty-five-mile straight shot. There were no clear directions or maps from jobs I held (local church pastor, photocopier salesman, not-for-profit director, seminary instructor, and lumber salesman), my marital status (married, divorced, remarried), and my life experiences (among them, a friend's suicide). My life more closely resembled a map from Portland to West Bowdin, Maine, traveling craggy, winding roads, with many alternate routes.

As I grew contemplative in my faith, questions arose as to how any of the things I had done fit into "*a*" wonderful plan for my life. Learning to see life as way opens answered that question.

You might want to draw a "map" of your life. Take a blank sheet of paper and write down some the important moments of your life. Put the "high" moments in the upper half of the sheet, the "low" ones below. Has your life followed a straight line? Does it move easily from one to the next? Did the high or low moments provide places where you could have followed another or a new direction—or did they point you on the same way?

Our lives reinforce the truth of a verse from Proverbs—"In all thy ways acknowledge him, and he shall direct thy paths." *Paths*—plural. The writer of Proverbs acknowledges that our lives don't have just one path. We are offered many paths as we follow the sacred compass.

PILGRIMS LIVE WITH IMAGINATION AND SPIRIT

Following the sacred compass calls us to live with imagination and spirit because there is not just one way to go, and we have no set map to follow. Way opens uniquely for each person. Our way unfolds as we move through life. The Inner Teacher uses our life experiences to show the way opening before us. Look at the life map you drew earlier. As you look at the highs and lows and in-betweens, how did particular experiences open a way for you? Do you, upon reflection, see God using them to move you in a certain direction, or away from a certain direction?

That's how spiritual direction works in John Irving's novel *A Prayer for Owen Meany*. Owen was a tiny, bizarre person with weirdly luminescent skin and the strangest, eeriest voice God ever gave anybody. Which is what Owen believed—that God *gave* him his stature, his voice, and all his other characteristics for a reason. Owen believed he was God's instrument.

His best friend, John Wheelwright, was a much more normal kid (if there really is any such creature). Wheelwright doubted God, life, and Owen's obsession with being God's instrument—

until Owen's death—when he saw God's purposes clearly. The difference between the two boys was that for Owen, the idea that God called him led him to a place where he could see the way opening, but John needed almost his entire childhood and young adulthood to find the thread of grace weaving its way through his life.

John and Owen's different experiences of the way opening were not based on their suitability for sainthood. Neither would qualify—especially Owen, who seemed to flaunt every rule of holiness. He was impure, indecent, and unfit by most standards for any sort of holy adoration. Yet Owen Meany was a saint because he lived as if he believed that God was real and knowable and had a direction for everybody—even a tiny boy/man with a wrecked voice.

This comforts me. Like Meany, am I flawed, confused, and doing my best with God's help to live a life of spiritual substance and holy obedience. Owen's failings were, for the most part, failings of the flesh, not of faith. In that he has good company in the Bible—David and his lusty heart, Noah and falling-down drunkenness after docking the ark. David and Noah were people doing their best to follow God's direction. And they were chosen to do God's work. God is funny that way—choosing the goofiest and weakest of us to accomplish divine purposes. Because of the role they played in God's work, David and Noah stand as exemplars of our potential God-directedness. They encourage us to see that way opens for us to follow God in the midst of life's messiness—including our self-made messiness.

Put your spiritual imagination to work: Why does God use you? What good qualities can you place at God's disposal? What quirks? Using our imagination and spirit enables us to see ourselves as pilgrims entrusted by God to do noble work.

PILGRIMS LEARN TO TRUST GOD

Trusting that God directs our paths teaches us to see the ways life opens. Our lives are filled with potential "a-ha" moments. Following our spiritual compass helps us see the "a-has." Trusting God also allows us to be real and genuine and authentic people, because trust helps us be more aware of the circumstances through which we pass. We see our flaws and frailties, and can still embrace the fact that we are people who hunger after God and are instruments of God.

Owen Meany knew, and John Wheelwright learned, the essence of living in a state of attention to the way opening as urged by mystic Isaac Penington. Penington said:

Know what it is to walk in the path of life. . . . It is that which groans, and which mourns; that which is begotten of God in you. . . . The true knowledge of the way, with the walking in the way, is reserved for God's child, for God's traveller. Therefore . . . don't strive to be any more than God has made you. Give God your will . . . and, sink down to the seed that God sows in the heart and let that grow in you.

I love the idea that "the true knowledge of the way, with the walking in the way, is reserved for God's child, for God's traveller." As I look at my life, I see one of motion. Though firmly rooted in the Midwest, as an adult I've lived in sixteen houses in two states, held fifteen full- or part-time jobs, and owned too many cars. Your life may be less frenetic than mine, but I'm sure that as you look over your history you'll see various movements in your life as well—careers, family, spiritual and physical changes. The movements all fit with the concept of way opening. Way opening implies motion; a moving along life's pilgrim way. What a winsome discovery.

PILGRIMS SEE GOD IN THE DETAILS

Pilgrimage shows us that every experience is one of discovering how way opens through the details of daily life. In an old Steve Martin comedy shtick, Socrates' faithful followers come with the news that he has been convicted of corrupting the youth of Athens and has been sentenced to drink hemlock, which he does—heroically and unafraid. When his followers ask him how he can face death so bravely, Socrates, played by Steve Martin, is startled. He asks what they mean. They're bewildered—doesn't he know that hemlock is poison? When they tell him, he's really upset. He proclaims, "It was always: 'Socrates, what is truth? Socrates, what is the nature of the good? Socrates, what should I order? Socrates, what are you having?' And not once did anyone ever say: 'Socrates, hemlock is poison!' " Aah, the details.

And yet that is where the will of God lies in our lives—in the details. What are some of the details that have revealed God to you?

- A smile?
- A tear?
- A scene from nature?
- A morsel of food?

God is at work in everything that shapes and moves and forms us. As Malcolm Muggeridge says:

Indeed, every true word ever uttered, every thought sincerely and lucidly entertained, every harmonious note sung or sounded, laughter flashing like lightning between the head and heart, human love in all its diversity binding together husbands and wives, parents and children, grandparents and grandchildren, and making of all mankind one family and our earth their home; the earth itself with its colours and shapes and smells, and its setting in a universe growing ever vaster and its basic components becoming ever more microscopic—seen with the eyes of Faith, it all adds up to a one-ness, an image of everlasting reality.

PILGRIMS TRAVEL TOGETHER

When we follow God's direction in our lives, we do not travel alone. Pilgrims travel in groups, giving each other strength. As spiritual pilgrims we are on this journey along with all of God's other children. Sometimes our paths converge. Other times they diverge. Regardless, we are not bereft of fellow travelers, other seekers of the Spirit. Traveling together and experiencing the joy of the journey are as much a part of pilgrimage as arriving at our destination. Camaraderie makes the trip special and gives strength in times of homesickness.

There is another way that we are not alone on our pilgrimage. This time, though, I am not talking about the other travelers who are making the journey with us. Rather, there is one with us who often goes unseen. Part of the role of heeding the sacred compass is to make sure that this one does not go unnoticed. God travels beside us, inside us, above us, around us, and watches over our souls. The Psalmist tells us:

> I lift up my eyes to the hills.
> From whence does my help come?
> My help comes from the LORD,

who made heaven and earth.
He will not let your foot be moved,
he who keeps you will not slumber.
Behold, he who keeps Israel
will neither slumber nor sleep.
The LORD is your keeper;
the LORD is your shade
on your right hand.
The sun shall not smite you by day,
nor the moon by night.
The LORD will keep you from all evil;
he will keep your life.
The LORD will keep
your going out and your coming in
from this time forth and for evermore.

This psalm reminds us that we are wrong if we think God's interest in us depends on our feeling that God is close by. God is our keeper—whether we feel God's care or not. When we say yes to God, we find ourselves in relationship. Love beckons us into love. We are called into relationship with one who cares for us so much that the hairs of our head are numbered (though in my case, that's not a very large number).

As we follow our sacred compass, we learn in deeper and deeper ways that God's care is steady and ongoing. We need not feel God's care to know it is working, any more than we need to feel gravity to keep us from sailing off into space. The law of God's ever-watchful presence is as surely in operation as are the natural laws of the universe that we take for granted.

Living into an increasing understanding of God's ever-presence is how we can pray along with Thomas Merton:

My Lord God, I have no idea where I am going. I do not see the road ahead of me. I cannot know for certain where it will end. Nor do I really know myself, and the fact that I think that I am following your will does not mean that I am actually doing so. But I believe that the desire to please you does in fact please you. And I hope I have that desire in all that I am doing. I hope that I will never do anything apart from that desire. And I know that if I do this, you will lead me by the right road though I may know nothing about it. Therefore will I trust you always though I may seem to be lost and in the shadow of death. I will not fear, for you are ever with me, and you will never leave me to face my perils alone.

Merton's words show us that a life of honest prayer is part of following the way that opens. What is honest varies from time to time, depending on our circumstances. Honest prayer will include some basics—an admission that we feel lost and can't see the way, letting God know that we desire direction, asking for pure motives in following the way, and stating, by and in faith, that God is with us and we want God to be with us. Use the details and circumstances of your life to shape your honest prayers. What ingredients would you combine to create an honest prayer for today? Are they different from what you would have used yesterday? If so, why? What does that teach you?

PILGRIMS ARE GRACED WITH GOD'S PRESENCE

God is with us, spreading grace over our lives. We, body and soul, are under the watchful eye of one who is ever vigilant. God cares for us more than we can know this side of heaven. While we are no freer from our share of life's disasters than anybody else is, we do have one with us who will never leave our side or end the loving watch over us.

The idea of life as a pilgrimage means that when we come to a fork in the road, we'll take it, as the great philosopher Yogi Berra said. We keep moving in trust. As we do so, we live into the reality that God speaks to us through every event of every day—every person we encounter, everything we do, and every moment we experience. As we follow our sacred compass, our job is to keep our ears, eyes, minds, and souls open to God so that we learn to perceive the ways our exterior experiences can influence our interior lives. God knows our circumstances. Some of us are blessed with set times of prayers and devotion; others are blessed with family and work obligations that fill every hour. Regardless, God speaks and guides us gently and according to our needs and situation.

Name some of the exterior things God uses to teach you. For me, God often uses things such as rides I take on my tractor or the people I watch around me when I walk downtown. My "tractor time" opens me up to an appreciation of God's creative work; people watching reminds me that I am surrounded by God's family even when, sometimes especially when, they don't look like me.

Busy at work or sitting still in a cathedral, God is ever with us.

PILGRIMS KEEP MOVING

We are a traveling people. We decide whether we travel as tourists or pilgrims. Tourists leave their footprints as monuments, while a pilgrim's footprints are a marker. William Faulkner said the difference between the two is that "a monument only says, 'At least I got this far,' while a footprint says, 'This is where I was when I moved again.' " Our sacred compass keeps us moving again—sometimes quickly, sometimes slowly, but always with a traveling companion or companions, seen and unseen.

Seeing ourselves as pilgrims and our lives as a pilgrimage changes us. To be pilgrims means that we are people who spend our lives going somewhere—in our case, going to God. Deep in our souls, we realize that, as an old hymn says, this world is not our home, we are just a-passin' through. To be a pilgrim is to answer Jesus' call to be his disciples—to follow him on the spiritual road.

This idea of life as pilgrimage is countercultural. Eugene Peterson, in his book *A Long Obedience in the Same Direction*, says that we live in a tourist society. We pass through life looking for attractive sights to visit and enjoyable experiences to partake of, and then we move on. As we move deeper into the life of the spirit, though, we grow into an understanding that faith is more than a tourist attraction. Faith is a journey. Sometimes faith is a slog. When we endeavor to walk the pilgrim path, we also discover that there is something in the attempt that makes life worth living. Faith stretches us. It deepens us. The grace of God enlarges our souls. We begin to live into the realization that God is with us through all of life—the ups, downs, and in-betweens—and we begin to relax into the comfort of that realization.

◆

Keeping to the touchstone of as way opens helps us to live more faithfully. We see that every path we've taken, every misstep we've made, every prayer we've uttered, whether it seemed to be answered or not, is part of our pilgrimage to the peace and fellowship and will of God. The sacred compass leads us on a pilgrimage toward divine life, love, and light. We put slavish servitude to step-by-step directions behind us and step boldly into the paths before us—confident that God welcomes our seeking, stumbling steps toward heaven.

TWO

LIVES THAT SPEAK
What We Are Saying to Others and Ourselves Along the Way

W E HAD JUST TAKEN OFF FROM MEMPHIS, headed toward Indianapolis, and we were bouncing all over the sky. I hate flying. My heart races, my palms are sweaty, I have difficulty breathing—and that's just at the airport. I've tried a variety of things to ease the pain of the plane. Whimpering with my eyes shut is not helpful. That night I did what I usually do: I put on my headphones and switched on a CD of *Fly Without Fear: Guided Meditations for a Relaxing Flight,* by Krs Edstrom.

Krs's voice is smooth, soft, and calming, but what really makes the CD effective is the way she calls attention to the very things I try to pretend aren't happening: sweaty palms, upset stomach, racing heart. She urges me to look at them, name them, and give them a number corresponding to my level of anxiety. When I do this, I usually find that my body tells me things aren't as bad as my head has made them out to be. That night, this routine worked—mostly—and listening to the CD reminded me of another phrase that relates to the sacred compass: "Let your life speak."

The original intent of this statement was for it to be an exhortation to a kind of quiet evangelism. This phrase urged Quakers to show God at work in their lives by doing more than just talking about their faith. To let your life speak was a rejoinder to "your actions speak so loudly, I can't hear what you're saying." But the phrase "let your life speak" also contains another gem of wisdom: that at the same time our lives are speaking to others, our lives are also speaking to us. The trick is to learn to listen to ourselves. I say "trick" because, as the writer Parker Palmer points out, today's culture teaches us to listen to everyone and everything but ourselves.

Changing our spiritual listening habits helps us hear ourselves. When we do that, we find that our lives speak to us about who we are, what our capabilities are, and what our purpose in life is in each season and situation. There are many ways of learning to listen to our lives, including:

- looking at them in light of what we understand through our faith
- searching Scripture
- praying
- and talking to spiritually wise friends.

Letting our lives speak helps us follow our way with integrity by showing us how to integrate body and soul. Krs's voice teaches me to hear what my body is telling emotionally and physically, and the sacred compass helps us trust our bodies to do the same for us spiritually. This deep listening allows us to see God's direction for how to respond to what we've heard. Understanding what our body—and our life—says moves us to face realistically the things that need doing.

OUR LIVES SPEAK THROUGH OUR BODIES

We don't often think of our bodies as carriers of spiritual truth, but an essential part of learning to let our lives speak is listening to what our bodies say about the situations life presents and the directions we feel led to go.

Consider how you feel when you're contemplating doing some new activity or going on an adventure:

- Do you feel drawn to it—almost compelled?
- Is your body relaxed as you think about it—or tense? Or both?
- Where do you feel these sensations—in your tight neck muscles, butterfly-filled stomach, tapping toe, or smiling face?

Such body wisdom, while often going unrecognized, deserves attention. As the poet Mary Oliver reminds us in her poem "Wild Geese," following our sacred compass does not mean that we have to be good or do a pilgrimage on our knees.

Instead we have to let what she calls the soft animal of our body "love what it loves."

I know the soft animal of my body often tells me things about what I love, as well as what I don't love (besides flying!). When I get sweaty, out of breath, and feel irritable for seemingly no reason, it means my blood sugar is probably low and I need to eat something. That's obvious body wisdom. But if I feel those sensations when I get up to speak or preach or teach, they usually mean something else. After years of experiencing such pre-speech syndromes, I know my body's telling me that I'm about to do something really important. My nervousness is a good thing; it alerts me that the task I'm undertaking deserves paying attention to.

We need to learn to listen to what our bodies tell us. After all, we are not just souls—just look in the mirror! We're imperfectly (at least most of us) shaped physical creatures. The spiritually astute reconnect with this wisdom, but many of us have lost the ability to listen to what our physicality tells us about both our bodies and our souls. Author Dan Wakefield says, "In trying to answer the question, 'How do we know when it's God?' I have come to trust the body over the mind; while conflicting messages rage in the head, the calmness or the agitation of the body has become my best guide." Wakefield's words are surprising, in some ways. We're a society that, while body conscious, is often body ignorant, perhaps because much of our activity is mechanized and removed from the physical reality of our selves.

I thought about this idea as some family members and I traveled to and around the Pacific Northwest for ten days. We flew to Chicago, entrained to Seattle, ferried to Victoria, British Columbia, and back to Seattle, entrained to Eugene, drove up the Oregon coast, and flew back home. It was quite a journey, filled with magnificent scenery, great times with friends and family, and the joy of seeing new things, such as sea lions swimming wild in the ocean. But no matter how we traveled, we were snug in air-conditioned comfort and our route was determined for us. The train followed the tracks. The ferry followed the shipping channels. The car followed the roads from Eugene to Florence and then up the coast. The plane followed air routes established by the Federal Aviation Administration. There was no physical meandering on planes, trains, ships, or roads.

This type of travel is unlike our way through life to God, which is probably one reason why our way to God is more of a hike than a tour. On a hike, we can stay on the road, walk the rails, swim a while, or just wander off the path and see what we want to see. We can nap in a meadow, climb a tree in the woods, or get lost. We feel sharp rocks under our feet and briars scratch us. A hike is not as safe and comfortable as a plane, train, ferryboat, or car. But we see and feel and learn things that we can't in any other way.

As we hike through life, we experience both the physical and spiritual joys and sorrows of the way. Our feet talk to us—as do our hearts, minds, and souls. They each help us determine the directions God wants us to take and the life activities we should pursue. Some of them may lead to making the world kinder, more loving, and more beautiful. Others may lead toward making ourselves kinder and more inwardly beautiful. As we learn to pay attention to what our bodies tell us about our soul's path, we relearn that we are not divided beings. We aren't solely souls or purely physical. We are connected. As we seek way opening for us, we learn that the body has as much to teach the soul as the soul does the body.

For starters, the way we care for our body when it tells us it needs food or rest teaches us that we also need to provide food and rest for our souls. We learn to nourish our souls by doing things that give them life:

- praying
- reading
- listening to music
- walking in nature

The list varies by soul, in the same way that food preferences or the need for a certain amount of sleep varies by body. Paying attention to our bodies shows us, oddly enough, that we need to tend our souls as well.

OUR LIVES SPEAK THROUGH OUR STORIES

Besides listening to our physical selves, there other ways to uncover what our lives are saying. One is to tell ourselves our faith stories—something that many of us don't do, probably because we assume we know our own stories since we're living them, after all. But the act of actually writing our spiritual stories provides amazing insight. Such stories show us the trajectory of our lives and souls. They help us see places where way opened for us. They show us the subtle hand of God resting upon us lightly or not so, through both the dramatic and everyday acts of our lives. They demonstrate the sacred compass in action.

There aren't any set rules for writing spiritual stories. Your story can be as brief or long as you want. If you're unsure where to start, pick one of the pivotal moments in your life, a time that you found life changing. You might begin by completing one of the following sentences:

- The most important lesson God taught me was . . .
- A faith crisis that helped me grow was . . .
- A gift God gave me was . . .
- A time I felt close to God was . . .

Another way to begin is to tell your story through your personal faith tradition. Write about why you follow the faith that you do. Are you Catholic by choice or birth or both? How have you arrived at the faith you now hold? Describe your path. As you think about your story, ask yourself:

- What is the title of your story?
- What would be your first line?
- What will come from your heart?

The goal is to get started. By telling your story to yourself, you get to open some parts of your life that have long had something to say.

If you find this kind of soulful storytelling helpful, you may want to go deeper and begin a spiritual autobiography. If you do, you'll find books like Nan Phifer's *Memoirs of the Soul: Writing Your Spiritual Autobiography* and Dan Wakefield's *The Story of Your Life: Writing a Spiritual Autobiography* helpful. Both are filled with exercises that will get your spiritual stories flowing.

OUR LIVES SPEAK THROUGH IMAGINATION

Writing is just one way of letting to your life speak. Other ways might better fit your personality and life. Sybil MacBeth came up with a way of praying in color (which is now a workshop and book by that name) during a time in her life when family and friends were dealing with a multitude of illnesses. She found no words for her prayers, and so took up pens and colored markers and began drawing. She added names and colors to the shapes she drew. Sybil says when she finished each drawing she saw each as a wordless act of holding her family and friends in prayer and commending them into God's care.

There are many ways to let our lives speak to us—intellectually, artistically, and aesthetically. Be open to ways that may be new to you—or ways that are old and may have fallen into disuse. As adults, many of us haven't taken up markers and paper in years and so the thought of praying in color may be intimidating or even frightening. But even though St. Paul urges us to put away childish things, some of the things of childhood that we've left behind—imagination, creativity, and play—help us let our lives speak in clearer tones. Perhaps that is partly why Jesus urged us to become like little children, so we'd return to that place of openness, wonder, and possibility.

OUR LIVES SPEAK THROUGH OUR INCLINATIONS

The Bible is full of images—the kingdom of God as tiny mustard seed or the safety of sitting under the shadow of God's wings. One recurring biblical image is the comparison of our lives to clay. I experienced that image in a new way one Christmas when our friend Carter got to talking with my wife, Nancy, about throwing pots. Nancy got a potter's wheel for Christmas that year and that set Carter and her off about how different clays felt and did different things while throwing them. Even though I was an art major, I didn't remember that there were different kinds of clay. Clay is clay, right? Wrong.

There's stoneware pottery clay, white clay, Raku clay, cone-5 mid-fire clay, porcelain clay, and . . . you get the idea. What I found interesting was their talking about what the clay *wanted* to do. One clay was hard to throw because it wanted to do this, while another was easier because it wanted to do that. Who knew clay *wanted* to do anything? I couldn't help but think about Isaiah 64, "O Lord, thou art our father; we are the clay, and thou our potter; we all are the work of thy hand." Yes, God is our potter, but it appears that the clay, according to Carter and Nancy, still has something to say. God asks a little earlier in Isaiah, "Does the clay say to him who fashions it, 'What are you making'? or 'Your work has no handles'?" Evidently, in some ways, the answer is yes.

Just like clay, we are easily molded in some ways and not in others. Another part of listening to our lives speak is to recognize these natural tendencies:

- Do you lean toward public ministry or private friendship?
- Do you prefer social justice marches or making donations to worthy causes?
- What do your life experiences teach you?
- How do your emotions and desires inform what you do—or don't do?

You are probably confident and able in some situations, but completely frazzled by others. Like the clay, we all function best when directed into situations and places where the traits God gave us are developed and shaped.

Of course, we do have to be careful to avoid using our clay-like qualities as an excuse for inaction or to avoid God's direction. Even Indian red clay, which is meant to be thrown on the wheel, doesn't start out as anything but a block of mud-like substance. To use Carter and Nancy's language, it doesn't *want* to do anything. But a good potter knows the clay and begins shaping it from a lump into something beautiful. And the shaping comes from the inside out—the potter's hands work inside the clay to form the outside, always drawing it upward and outward.

The experience of a fellow I know named Stan Zarowin showed me the truth of this idea. He told me, "A significant time [for me] was when I became clear that I should become involved in facilitating antiviolence workshops in prisons. I don't particularly like doing that work, but I feel compelled. I've done it [now] for some twenty years."

I don't know Stan well—just through our time together in a newly formed worship-sharing group—but my experience is that this compulsion reveals his true nature. I see him as a man of peace and action. I daresay that following his inclinations led him to his true self—a truer self than he would have found had he taken an easier way or ignored his inclinations. The divine potter drew him upward and outward.

OUR LIVES SPEAK THROUGH OPPORTUNITIES

One way of testing what kind of clay we are and what we're meant to do is by placing ourselves "in the way" of opportunities for growth and experience. Life and God offer us all sorts of opportunities—from campus internships, committee work, community volunteer work to short-term mission trips, elder hostels, and travel—that lead deeper into discernment. Such experiences may confirm that something is to be our life's vocation or, just as helpfully, demonstrate that it's not for us. A writer friend of mine, Nan Phifer, had a confirming experience during a writing workshop:

> I remember a time when I was giving a workshop in a Methodist Church in a town on the southern coast of Oregon. I looked over the heads of a group of remarkably responsive writers to see the Pacific Ocean spread blue and vast. *This is what I am meant to do*. I felt certain and fulfilled.

When you place yourself "in the way," take time to gauge how the opportunity molds you. Ask yourself:

- ◆ Does what you're doing feel right?
- ◆ Does it feel forced?
- ◆ What does this opportunity teach you?
- ◆ Does it give you life—or drain it?

Such opportunities are a time of teaching and learning. Use them to gain new spiritual insight and check your sacred compass.

OUR LIVES SPEAK IN DREAMS

Paying attention to our dreams is another way of listening to our lives speak. Understanding dreams as spiritual leadings has deep biblical roots. Jacob dreamt of a stairway to heaven. In his dream, he heard a promise to him from God—a promise that completely redirected his life. King Nebuchadnezzar had a dream that only Daniel could interpret. As the dream was one that challenged the king's power and rule, Daniel was the only one who dared interpret it (not many kings look kindly upon those who threaten their reign). Daniel told him that the dream meant the king would be brought low until he recognized that God, not himself, was in charge. Pharaoh's dreams sprung Joseph from jail and set him up as a leader in the land of Egypt; the Magi were warned in a dream not to return to Herod, and thereby helped spare the life of the infant Christ.

We do not put as much stock in dreams as our ancient spiritual ancestors did, and so many of us miss a rich way of letting our lives speak to us. When we dream, the world falls away and that which is subconscious bubbles to the surface. Sometimes God's word for us makes its way out to us in dreams that teach us, if we let them.

A Mennonite pastor, Ryan, told me of three times God used dreams to speak to him. Each, he said, occurred during times of great anxiety, and each was about something different. One of them came when the church conference he belonged to at the time was preparing to remove two congregations from membership for having homosexual members. He was opposed to the conference's proposed action and argued with leadership and tried various political gambits to block them.

One night I was unable to sleep, angry and anxious. I had recently been studying the Book of Jonah and had noticed that God would not allow the sailors to sail out of the storm to avoid throwing Jonah overboard. The sailors were compelled to go against their conscience, not realizing God had a bigger plan—a rescuing fish—in store. As I tossed and turned in bed, an inner voice suddenly and clearly said to me, "I have a fish to save those congregations." I am not a person who has visions, but this was as compelling as anything I had ever felt. I immediately relaxed, assured that even if the worst were to happen—the two congregations being thrown overboard—God still had a fish to rescue them. The next day I felt compelled to call two conference leaders with whom I had had heated exchanges and tell them, calmly and peacefully, about my experience. A couple weeks later, when the conference met, the leadership expressed openness to discussing other possible avenues. Respectful and humble discussion ensued. Friendships were restored.

Another friend told me about receiving guidance in a dream. "It very vividly warned me against doing something," she said. "Unfortunately, I didn't listen."

"There are many voices in the night," says Old Testament scholar Walter Brueggemann, "not all of them noble. Among them, however, is the voice of the holy God, who 'plucks up and tears down' what we have trusted, who 'plants and builds' what we cannot even imagine . . . the community of faith has known— and trusted—from the outset [that] there is something outside our controlled management of reality which must be heeded. Sometimes that something turns out to be a miracle of new life."

OUR LIVES SPEAK TO AUTHENTICITY

Listening to our lives speak is vital because such listening leads us to our authentic selves. There have been times I pretended to be somebody I wasn't—Sky King, Roy Rogers, the Lone Ranger, Batman. Pretending to be somebody else is a part of growing up. But it is something we generally need to outgrow as an adult (though it is fun to dress up and pretend sometimes). And we usually do. Most of us are happy to be who we are and don't wish we were somebody else, except, sometimes, when it comes to matters of faith.

While we want to walk close to God and be the people we sense we are called to be, when we meet a person who is obviously a person of faith, we begin to feel somehow inadequate. It's as if our faith was somewhat incomplete. "If only . . . " we think. "If only I were more like that person."

We are surrounded by many living examples of faith. We encounter people every day who point the way to life and God. They are examples of godliness in daily life. Yet, for all the good they do and faith they have, that is all they are to be to us— examples. We can learn from them, but we cannot be them. Their lives may speak to our spirits, saying things such as:

- Be more patient.
- Take time for prayer.
- Have a generous spirit.
- Love the unlovely.

But we have to remember God does not want us to try to be just like them. Instead, we have to learn to be people of faith as the people we are—flaws and all. We are called to be the distinct individuals God made us to be, to serve God as ourselves, not as imitations of somebody else.

Theologian Martin Buber said that learning to be ourselves, as God meant us to be, might be what makes up our true life's work. He wrote, "All [of us] have access to God, but each has a different access. [Our] great chance lies precisely in

[our] unlikeness. God's all-inclusiveness manifests itself in the infinite multiplicity of the ways that lead to him, each of which is open to [one] person."

Buber illustrated what he meant using a story of a rabbi named Zusya. A short time before his death, the rabbi said, "In the world to come I shall not be asked: 'Why were you not Moses?' I shall be asked: 'Why were you not Zusya?'" What Buber and Zusya tell us is that we need to let the sacred compass point us to who we are meant to be. We need to ask the question, *What does it mean to be me?*

The answer won't come gift-wrapped and dropped from heaven, especially during the times when we sense our imperfections. How can anybody less than perfect truly follow God's holy path? St. Therese wrote, "Perfection consists in being [who] God wants us to be." We needn't worry if we've reached spiritual perfection. Instead, we must try some things we've witnessed from the folks we consider models of true faith. If I see someone whose prayer life inspires me, I can first test my soul by asking, "Is this telling me to pray more?" My sacred compass will most likely say yes, and I'll sense that answer in both my heart and head.

But if I take the next step and say, "She gets out of bed and begins her prayer life at 5:30 every morning, praying until 7:00. I'll do the same," chances are that my compass will begin to jiggle and the direction arrow will wobble. Early rising is not a practice that fits me. I hate early mornings. I need my oatmeal

(Quaker, of course) and coffee before I can function. I may also have the spiritual version of Attention Deficit Disorder—I have a difficult time staying focused on long sessions of prayer. My compass's jiggling shows me that I should go another direction. Yes to more prayer, no to early rising and extended prayer sessions. I can then ask how to achieve my goal. My sacred compass stays centered on spiritual true north when I pray more by praying more *often*—short seasons of prayer throughout the day. When people or situations pop into my mind or soul, I pray—while in meetings, working at my desk, or driving my car.

That's how the sacred compass works. Take a reading when you're inspired by a person of faith. Set your direction and keep your eye on the needle. If it wobbles, try another direction. As you align with the compass's direction, you'll find soulful satisfaction in growing spiritually. Don't be discouraged when you find one path doesn't work for you. As Thomas à Kempis said, "Lose not thy confidence of making progress in godliness; there is yet time, the hour has not passed."

OUR LIVES SPEAK THROUGH SEASONS

What our life says about God's direction differs when we're nineteen from when we're ninety. God's guidance is fitted to our ability—spiritually and physically—in each season of life. Sometimes the spirit may be willing, while the flesh is weak.

At others, the flesh may be strong, while the spirit is not in the greatest shape. College, career, marriage, living single, raising children, raising pets, caring for our adult parents, and retirement may open new ways of service never before imagined.

The novelist Vinita Hampton Wright talked to me about the seasons of her life and the leadings that accompanied them. During her twenties, she experienced a strong leading to do mission work outside the United States. "That desire was confirmed," she said, "by an appointment [to the mission field]. I knew—despite my parents' protests—that it was the right step. The experience itself—two years teaching in Jordan—was not easy, but definitely confirmed that I had made the right decision."

Now, years later, she has been following a new leading. "I recently decided to go back to editorial work full-time," she said, "which will be hard on my writing career, but the situation in my marriage requires it, and I am at peace with the decision and the difficulty it will bring."

When I asked her how she listened to her life in making such a determination, she replied:

When I needed to make some difficult decisions in my writing career, I talked to a very wise friend in the field, also well-respected in the industry and familiar with me and my work. Her advice had a strong impact on that decision. Most of the time, my decisions are determined by deep desire, along with opportunity, along with underlying principle or reason for the decision. My long-term commitments, such as my marriage, also weigh in heavily on any other decision. Although I don't ask friends to help me make a decision, I usually want to hear what they have to say about a situation. Especially my close friends, who know me well, can help me see more clearly.

Vinita listened to her life speak throughout the various seasons of her life. Where one calling was clearly correct for her twenties, a new direction emerged for this time of her life. Her life, and her obedience to her callings, reminds us that we don't go to God in a straight line. Our compass may lead over the spiritual river and through the holy woods as to our Father's house we go. The terrain of our trek will vary. We can check our compass to see if, as the seasons change, we need to change direction, too. We can calibrate our compass by assessing our physical ability, spiritual state, financial needs and abilities, intellectual knowledge and curiosity, vocational opportunities, heart's calling, and any number of things that change as we move through life. We can determine what has changed and what has stayed the same. The answers will lead us aright.

OUR LIVES SPEAK THROUGH OUR HEARTS

Another way we listen to our lives speak is by paying attention to our heart. When I was a local pastor, my wife, Nancy, developed a series of supposedly subtle hand signals that she flashed me while I preached. I guess she thought I needed more than divine direction. One sign was putting her hands together and slowly drawing them apart to say, "Slow down; you're talking too fast." Another was an unwrapping motion, which meant, "You're slurring your words and may be having a sugar low, so unwrap a piece of candy and pop it in your mouth!" The one she used most was to gently tap her heart, meaning, "Stop talking from your head and speak from your heart."

That was the best sign, and it can be a good way for us to learn to listen to our lives speak. We need to listen to our hearts. Debra Farrington says that we need hearts that are:

- wise
- prayerful
- attentive
- learning
- open
- imaginative
- thoughtful
- engaged

- ◆ patient
- ◆ active

Those are powerful adjectives, especially when applied to the heart. What would it mean for you to have a wise heart? How does an attentive heart feel? Can you imagine an imaginative heart? Thoughtful hearts, engaged hearts, and learning hearts will be different for every person.

We each already have a heart with those adjectives at work in some degree. You might add descriptors to your heart's list. As we learn to cultivate the type of heart described by these words, and as we learn to listen to that heart, we will find a deep way to listen to our lives speak. We often lean heavily on our intellect, but, as Farrington reminds us, in the life of going to God, "Wise heads are good. Wise hearts are essential."

OUR LIVES SPEAK THROUGH OUR VOICES

I spent time at a writer's asylum (an apt phrase for a gathering of writers if ever there was one) in Minnesota one summer. One of our group exercises was to name the voices rattling around inside our heads. We then counted them. One person said she had five. Another said one hundred. Another finally blurted out "Legion," referring to the story in the fifth chapter of Mark's Gospel where Jesus meets the demoniac living in the caves and tombs in Gerasenes. In the story, Jesus asks this troubled man what his name is, and he replies, "My name is Legion . . . for we are many." When Jesus casts the demons out, the man no longer is tormented by the many voices inside him. "Of course," said one writer, "his writing career was then ruined." We laughed, but acknowledged the truth of the voices inside us and talked at length about how to determine our truest voice.

Defining our truest voice doesn't mean shutting out all the other voices. They are all a part of us. We honor them and allow them to inform us. We just can't let them get out of hand. I know that when I set out to find direction, I am confronted by voices of authority that come from outside me (even if they are inside my head). I hear my father, mother, boss, board of directors, and sometimes my grandmother, who wonders if I'll ever get a real job. Sometimes the voices are helpful. At other times, they're scolding. Beside those voices, I hear others. Some are societal—telling me I should volunteer more because I know our local Habitat for Humanity could use my help on Saturday. Other voices tell me I could promote the books I've written and sell more copies if I'd travel and speak more. Still others say I'd have whiter teeth if I used brightening strips. All of these voices inside and out urge me to follow certain paths and make certain choices.

I need to cut through the clutter of the other voices and listen for just two—the voice of my life speaking and the voice of God. When I do that, I hear amazing things. Like Kaylin Haught did, in her off-beat, reverent/irreverent way, when she

> asked God if it was okay to be melodramatic
> and she said yes
> I asked her if it was okay to be short
> and she said it sure is
> I asked her if I could wear nail polish
> or not wear nail polish
> and she said honey
> she calls me that sometimes
> she said you can do just exactly
> what you want to
> Thanks God I said
> And is it even okay if I don't paragraph
> my letters
> Sweetcakes God said
> who knows where she picked that up
> what I'm telling you is
>   Yes Yes Yes

Count and name some of your interior voices. Can you identify the ones that are holding you back from listening to your true life with God? Which ones lead you to God saying, "Yes, yes, yes"?

OUR LIVES SPEAK THROUGH OUR DAYS

One way to practice listening for God's "Yes, yes, yes," is to ask yourself what you feel God's been saying to you over the past twenty-four hours. Review your day and probe it for what you think the day has been telling you. Talk with God about what you feel you're hearing. You might want to use prayer, quiet listening, journaling, chatting with a spiritual friend, or going for a walk to explore listening to God this way. There are many ways to practice listening to God—choose the ways that work for you.

◆

Letting our lives tell us what it knows about our values and truths as illumined by God's compass points to way opening into blessed, deep communion with God. If we are ever to discover the life that God has called us to—to walk where "way opens"—we need to listen to what our lives are saying. This listening helps us develop patterns of discernment that guide us throughout our lives.

When we listen, our lives speak and tell us that *this* fits and *that* doesn't. They confirm God's direction for us. As careful listeners to our lives, we can sift the honest from the dishonest, the wise choice from the good choice, and then live into the decision that fits our leadings, lives, and sacred compass. Listening to our lives speak leads us to a satisfying new way of being. It is a way of being that, as British zoologist Anna Bidder found, "is to me a source of love and gratitude and strength far deeper even than joy and happiness."

THREE
PAYING ATTENTION
Seeing the Signs on the Way

P EOPLE HAVE A HARD TIME FINDING OUR HOME. Our house sits 1,500 feet off the road and is nestled back in a wood. Also, house numbers in the country are few and far between, and they're on the mailboxes, not the houses. And the mailboxes, like the houses, are few and far between. So, to make finding us easier, Nancy and I put a sign that says, "Welcome to Ploughshares Farm," at the end of our long lane. If people look for the sign, they have a good chance of making their way to our home. That is, if they know to look for the sign.

LEADINGS START IN THE SOUL

Following our sacred compass is like hunting for a house down a country lane—we get the general direction, but need to learn to look for the signs. "Take heed of the promptings of Truth and Love, for those are the leadings of God," urged the first Quaker, George Fox. *Leadings* is the word that Friends use to describe direction or guidance coming from the Spirit of God. Divine direction, God's guidance, spiritual opportunity, and revelation are intimately tied into following the sacred compass.

A leading can be something as simple as the time Nancy and I stood in the checkout line at the local grocery store, our cart well loaded. Our three sons lived at home at the time and they went through food quickly. In front of us was a member of our meeting, who also had three sons. Her cart held a few essentials. A single mother, she was between jobs and doing her best to get by. I felt a prompting inside me. *By almost any standards, you are rich*, the voice said. *What should you do?* Then I remembered Jesus' words, "For I was hungry and you gave me food, I was thirsty and you gave me something to drink." I looked at Nancy, she nodded, and I tapped our friend on the shoulder. "Nancy and I would like to buy your groceries, if you'll allow us," I said so only she could hear. A look of relief filled her eyes and she nodded yes. As we three left the grocery, she said "Thanks. I have a lead on a job and this will really help tide us over until it comes through." That was the last thing ever said about this incident between us.

It wasn't that I suddenly became a saint there in the grocery store. The story is not about me being a good guy, but rather how, at least in that instance, I listened to the prompting of love—and responded. In doing so, I was helped more than my friend was—my soul was enlarged as my compassion for neighbors less well off than me became more than just some intellectual understanding. It became an exercise of faith. As Noel Paul Stookey, better known as Paul of Peter, Paul, and Mary, says, leadings are "an amplification of character, a step beyond expectations, usually in the spirit of giving or at the very least being a witness for righteousness."

While this was a small leading to the prompting of love, it also shows something else. Nancy had the same leading, and so did our friend, in a different way. Leadings can come to us individually and they can come to us corporately. Jesus said, "For where two or three are gathered in my name, there am I in the midst of them." All of life, and everything in the world around us, is sacred and imbued with the possibility of Christ's being there—including checkout lines at grocery stores. So, while we were two miles from our meetinghouse, three Friends stood together in the presence of Christ. Two had a leading to give. One had a leading to receive. In following that leading, a blessing fell on each of us.

Paying attention to our interior leadings alerts us to God's company around and within us. The leadings remind us to live the prayer of St. Patrick:

God be in my head, and in my understanding;
God be in my eyes, and in my looking;
God be in my mouth, and in my speaking;
God be in my heart, and in my thinking;
God be at my end, and at my departing.

LEADINGS BEGIN WITH GOD'S PROMPTING

As we begin to pay attention to the signs of such promptings in our heads, hearts, and speaking, we learn to discern them as motions of the Spirit in our lives.

Leadings are easy to miss because they're often subtle. Blogger Tatiana Harrison wrote to me that, for her, a leading usually "starts as a sudden urge to do something . . . kind of a 'spiritual itch.'"

Some signs of leading include sensations of

- love
- caring
- beauty
- persistence
- rightness
- feeling in harmony with God
- surrendering of our wills to God

These feelings manifest themselves in different ways to different people. My vision of what is beautiful might be far different from yours. And what I may perceive as nagging could be persistence to you. Ask yourself how you would know a leading was "right" or "in harmony with God." What clues tell you that a leading is true? True leadings take us to a place where we want to know more—a place where we can say with Christina Rossetti:

Speak, Lord, for your servant hears.
Grant me ears to hear
eyes to see,
a will to obey,
heart to love;
then declare what you will,
reveal what you will,
command what you will,
demand what you will.

LEADINGS OFTEN CALL US TO ACTION

Sometimes leadings are big—calls to action and responses to promptings of truth. When Rosa Parks stayed seated on December 1, 1955, in Montgomery, Alabama, she responded to a leading to speak truth to power. Most of us never experience leadings on such a national scale, but following any leading at all can be big to us, and to God. Career changes or moving to a new city aren't trifles. That was true for my next-door neighbor (one half-mile down the road!), Sylvia Graves. One recent leading was big for her, her husband, and the international community.

Sylvia retired after working thirty-four years as a schoolteacher and principal. For the first six months of retirement, she got their material possessions in order. She and her husband, Dale, moved from their big house to a smaller house next door that had belonged to her parents. She enjoyed the time off but was "beginning to feel restless to do something else, find a job that was helpful to others and not just centered on my own well-being."

At that time, a large Quaker organization was going through major staff changes. This national and international ministry and publishing organization needed fresh leadership. Sylvia has had a long history with this group, having served on various boards and committees. She felt a leading to meet with some of the board members. "What can I do to help?" she asked. The answer came in a few days when the search committee asked her to become the interim general secretary of the organization. "I had prayed all along that I would hear God when He called but had no idea that He would call me here," she says. That interim position led to a permanent role as the group's general secretary.

Sylvia's story points us to another aspect of leadings. We may not always know where they're leading at the time, but God does. Sylvia knew it was time to retire, but that's all she knew. She didn't retire to become interim general secretary of a vast organization—at least as far as she knew. But as African Quaker John Muhanji told her, "God knew and He was getting you ready."

LEADINGS SHOW THE WAY OPENING

Following our leadings, big and small, is integral to following our sacred compass. Leadings are the signs that show us how and where way is opening. Sometimes they're obvious—someone needs help with groceries or an organization needs the skills you have and you're in a place and time of life to help. Others are less so, such as the time I visited St. John's University in Minnesota and decided to take the back way from my apartment to the main campus. Using the brochure "Saint John's Arboretum Trails Map," which showed a way through the woods, some grassland, the nature preserve, and over a footbridge, I began. A nice black trail marked the way. On the map. I walked to where I thought I'd find a sign for the trailhead, but there was no sign. Or nice black trail. There was just tall grass. So I scouted for something resembling a trail, lowered my eyes, and saw trampled grass. In I went. Fifty feet later, I broke out of the grass and found myself on a broad path through the woods. The path didn't stay broad, though. When the path came out of the woods, I was back into grassland and had to look for a new narrow track. The narrow trail stayed narrow all the way to the footbridge leading across the lake (which was obvious) and then turned into a wide path through the woods leading up to campus.

In the same way that I had to look for subtle signs along the way on that walk, so, too, do we have to pay attention to the subtle signs of leadings in our lives. Quaker writer George Fox urges us to pay attention to the promptings of love and truth. But this is not always easy to do.

Many other Friends have written wisely about testing leadings or signs of leading. I've adapted some of them in the sections below, adding some of my own.

LEADINGS COME FROM WITHIN

One sign of a true leading is that it comes from within. Often, as George Fox noted, it begins with a prompting or motion toward love, like the leading I felt in the grocery store or Sylvia felt upon retirement, or what Tatiana calls an "itch." This prompting is usually a gentle nudge, not a shove or slap in the face. It might look like the path through slightly trampled grass. A leading comes with a sense of heightened spiritual sensitivity inside you that says, *Something is going on that's worth paying attention to.*

LEADINGS ARE OFTEN BEAUTIFUL

Another sign is that a leading is often a thing of beauty. It may be an overwhelming beauty, but is beautiful nonetheless. I used to wonder why angels' first words to people they encountered in the Bible were, "Be not afraid." Perhaps it has something to do with the awesome beauty the angels possessed from living in God's presence. Leadings may be that way, too—terrifyingly beautiful. We may not understand what we're seeing, but are awed by its effect. Other leadings may be subtler, but are no less beautiful. As Caroline Graveson points out:

God is in all beauty, not only in the natural beauty of earth and sky, but in all fitness of language and rhythm, whether it describes a heavenly vision or a street fight, a

Hamlet or a Falstaff, a philosophy or a joke: in all fitness of line and colour and shade, whether seen in the Sistine Madonna or a child's knitted frock: in all fitness of sound and beat and measure, whether the result be Bach's Passion music or a nursery jingle. The quantity of God, so to speak, varies in the different examples, but His quality of beauty in fitness remains the same.

LEADINGS ARE PERSISTENT

Persistence is another mark of a leading. The sacred compass does not take us to the "leading of the month club"—we won't be led to do one thing one day and the complete opposite the next. As Tatiana Harrison told me:

If the urge isn't something that has to be done immediately (it's never been so far), then I wait on it at least a couple of days to see what happens. Sometimes the urge will go away completely, which usually means it was just my ego wanting me to act nobly or for other people to think that I am a good, charitable person. But if the urge sticks around and increases in intensity, and if the action it's pointing towards becomes clearer and sharper, I'll know it's something God is calling me to do. I think the hardest part about discernment is that one has to be both impulsive *and* patient at the same time. If one is not impulsive, one can dismiss the leading as just another thought or shrug it off. But if one is not patient, one may follow the leading at the wrong time, or follow something that isn't even a leading at all!

Leadings may hang around the edges of our consciousness, reminding us of their presence while we drive or dine or do the dishes. They hang around, never quite disappearing, even difficult or seemingly unpleasant ones that we wish would go away! That's how I experienced a leading I'd been given to form a new worship-sharing group.

I'd been wrestling—and that's a good biblical word when it comes to dealing with stuff from God (see Jacob)—with this leading for three years. It was stronger at some times, weaker at others. But my leading was ever present, even when I tried to dismiss it. When I got into the serious work of writing this book on discernment, the leading emerged stronger than ever. I argued with God, "But I don't have the time." "Are you serious about discernment," God seemed to ask in response, "or just wanting to write about it?" Then a wise friend called and invited me to lunch to talk about some substantive spiritual matters. Over lunch, I told her about this leading. She said that I should stop running from it, and she even offered to help. So she and I issued an invitation to some people we thought might be interested in a worship group based on theological hospitality. I posted the invitation on my blog. Now, thanks to the Spirit's persistent work with me, a group meets twice monthly at our house for worship and deep spiritual sharing.

LEADINGS REQUIRE WAITING TIME

In addition to persistence, a period of waiting is also part of a leading (though God may hope that everybody else moves faster than I did!). We may want to rush ahead, but if we do, we risk missing signs along the way. When people rush into decisions, Quakers say they ran ahead of their leading—they outpaced the way God wanted them to go. Waiting, sometimes even long, painful periods of waiting, is needed to test a leading's integrity. As George Fox wrote, "Be patient and still in the power and still in the light that doth convince you, keep your minds unto God. . . . If you sit still in the patience which overcomes in the power of God, there will be no flying."

LEADINGS FILL US WITH JOY

We may also want to move ahead quickly because a leading fills us with joy. Though the great writer and theologian Frederick Buechner says, "The vocation for you is the one in which your deep gladness and the world's deep need meet—something that not only makes you happy but that the world needs to have done," we must make sure that our deep gladness or joy comes from God and not from our own will. There's much that brings us gladness, and there's much that the world needs done, but part of testing a leading through waiting is determining whether we are the person to meet that need. Has God called us to a task—or are we calling ourselves?

We may want to move quickly because events seem to be pressing us to action—we feel danger around us, there's no time to wait, and we must act. Perhaps we think of the words of contemporary martyr Dietrich Bonhoeffer, "When Christ calls a man he bids him come and die." We feel urgency to take action, but Bonhoeffer's words overstate the concept behind following the sacred compass.

Certainly, a prompting from God might lead to martyrdom, or it might mean a death to self. The question is if we are following God because way has truly opened for us to do so, or if laying ourselves on the altar of self-martyrdom is the result of some deep masochistic need. One way to find the answer is to test for the sense of joy. If we feel called, regardless of any possible emotional or even physical death the action may cause, there will be joy in surrendering to God. This joy in death seems paradoxical, but it is nonetheless real and is often something we can only know when we experience it.

LEADINGS BRING CALMNESS

Leadings are often accompanied by a sense of calmness. Sometimes this calmness is one of complete, soulful peace. At other times, it is a preternatural stillness like the one before the proverbial storm. Regardless, calmness comes in no small part because of assurance that this is the direction God wants us to go. We are calm because in a spiritual sense, if not a physical one, we are choosing life—life under God's direction, and life abundant and soulfully full. As spiritual director Patricia Loring says:

The central issue is always, "Where is the Spirit leading you?" If God sets before us every day the choice of Life and Death and says, "Choose Life!" (Deut. 30:19–29), where is Life? Biblically, it is in love of and obedience to God; "staying close to the Root," as earlier Friends might have said. It may not always be gaiety, song and dance, or even snuggling babies; but neither will it be grim duty. It will be the place that touches the "quick"—an old word for where the life is in oneself: life answering Life. One of the traditional Quaker tests of the authenticity of a leading has been, "Is there Life in it?"

If there is life in the leading, there will be calmness as well.

LEADINGS GIVE US POWER

Leadings also come with power. That's a thought that may make us uncomfortable, especially when we think of the truism that power corrupts. But in this case, the power is far from corrupting. Instead, it's *em*powering. It's a power that enables us to live out the leading. The Bible abounds with examples of this type of power, such as when the prophet Isaiah is overwhelmed by a vision of the Lord. At first, he laments, "Woe is me! For I am lost; for I am a man of unclean lips, and I dwell in the midst of a people of unclean lips; for my eyes have seen the King, the LORD of hosts!" After Isaiah says this, God directs an angel to cleanse Isaiah's lips. When his lips are cleansed, Isaiah hears God asking, "Whom shall I send, and who will go for us?" Isaiah answers, powerfully, "Here am I! Send me." Isaiah's words minister to us today, imbued as they were with a power he did not have until he followed God's direction. God offers us power to live out our leadings, but we must be willing to receive the power offered and use it well and wisely in God's service.

LEADINGS HELP US CONFRONT OUR WEAKNESS

Leadings often take us to a place where we face our frailties and failings. Isaiah says he's a man of unclean lips. Moses says his frailty is even greater. When God calls Moses to lead the Israelites out of bondage, Moses says, "Oh, my LORD, I am not eloquent, either heretofore or since thou hast spoken to thy servant; but I am slow of speech and of tongue." While some have made this out to be Moses throwing an excuse at God (plagues, pursuing armies, whiny Israelites, and having to live on manna, whatever that was), another way of looking at the story is to see Moses' honesty about his limitations. Who is he to be God's mouthpiece against Pharaoh? "Then the LORD said to [Moses], 'Who has made man's mouth? Who makes him dumb, or deaf, or seeing, or blind? Is it not I, the LORD? Now therefore go, and I will be with your mouth and teach you what you shall speak.'"

As with Moses, it is sometimes precisely because of our weaknesses and lack of ability that God calls us. In obeying our call, we learn to trust God and lean on God for strength. We become meek in the face of the leading. Our faith expands to meet the challenge God has laid before us. We move forward in a power that is more than our own.

LEADINGS BRING CLARITY

With all true leadings, we receive increasing clarity as we obey what God tells us. Clarity comes more readily if we are willing to do what our leading tells us to do. Clarity also comes with a sense of freedom from any burden. We feel that nothing is holding us back or down. We are free to move forward. Our soul has a clearness that comes from God. As George Fox put it, "I'm glad I was here. Now I'm clear. I'm fully clear."

LEADINGS NEVER GO AGAINST GOD'S TEACHINGS

In addition to the welcome sign at the end of our lane, Nancy and I have another sign on our property. Well, Nancy denies any ownership of it. It sits about three-fourths of the way down the long lane, is printed in stark black and white with a red border, and contains a list of forbidden activities. The sign was a gift from an old friend and is a copy of the sign that sat in the driveway of his farm before he and his wife moved to more maintenance-free quarters in the city. Some of the forbidden activities include smoking, spitting, innuendo, inyoufronto, and importing zucchini. They're all a joke (except the importing zucchini part—I'm seriously opposed to zucchini). It's fun to watch people stop their cars and get out to read the sign. Some smile. Some shake their heads, certain they are at the home of a crazy man.

We do have other signs, too, because of the acres of prairie grass and thousands of trees we've planted. They say things such as, "No Hunting," "No Motorized Vehicles," "Do Not Disturb Wildlife." These signs are serious and tell people who come on to our property—invited or not—how to respectfully behave while here. They are a literal how way should open—and say that way will never open for them to do any of those forbidden things.

In a similar way, in the life of the spirit we can be sure that way will never open to break God's laws. A leading will never lead us to murder or steal or do harm to another. It may lead us to break human laws—to perform an act of civil disobedience, for example—but never divine ones.

In addition to ensuring we are following God's laws, we need to check our leadings against the fruits of the spirit listed in the book of Galatians. Do our leadings demonstrate:

- love
- joy
- peace
- patience
- kindness
- generosity
- faithfulness
- gentleness
- self-control

If we think we're being led to be intemperate, such as to flip off that crazy driver weaving in and out on the freeway, there's a pretty good chance our leading is coming from someplace other than God. But if we sense love, joy, peace, patience, kindness, generosity, faithfulness, gentleness, and self-control behind and within our leadings, we can trust that we should follow them. God's precepts are pure—and they will speak to the pure in us.

LEADINGS FIT OUR TEACHABILITY

Will we all have the same leading about the same issue? Perhaps. But often we don't. That's because Christ, our Inner Teacher, knows our teachability. The Spirit works with us where we are and within our own capacities for growth. Yes, God might stretch us. We will probably feel such spiritual stretching most when we're lead in a way that others are not. But as Isaiah says, "I am the LORD your God, who teaches you for your own good, who leads you in the way you should go." *You*. In *your* way. God will not teach anyone else in your way; everyone is taught differently.

I turned eighteen at the height of the Vietnam Conflict. This meant I was supposed to register for the draft, which I did. Since I was a Quaker, I had the choice of signing up as a conscientious objector, but I couldn't. At that time I was ambivalent about war. Four of my uncles served in the military, and my mother's father fought in the Spanish-American War, yet I didn't feel led to that same way. I had been accepted into college and knew that as long as I kept my grades up I wouldn't have to decide whether or not to go to war for at least four years. So I registered and got my student deferment.

My friend Bob Gosney, who I met in seminary a few years later, found his way opening very differently. After initially not registering for the draft, he registered and applied for conscientious-objector status. He felt his participation in war went against his call to live in love and with nonviolence toward others, so he acted to keep himself out of the war. But Bob's application for conscientious-objector status was denied, and he refused induction into the military. He didn't flee to Canada to avoid prosecution, but rather stayed and took his lumps. He found himself in federal district court facing a five-year prison sentence and a ten thousand dollar fine. However, the Selective

Service System had the court case dismissed and reconsidered his application. He was found to be a conscientious objector and served two years of alternate service working at a state institution for mentally handicapped people.

Mark Peterson, now my son-in-law, found way opening for him in a still different way. His draft lottery number was high enough that he was in no danger of being drafted. But he was raised Lutheran, and as he looked over his life's and faith's call, he felt led to serve. This call is consistent with the two-kingdom theology (we are citizens of two kingdoms—the kingdom of heaven and the kingdom of earth that sometimes needs to take up arms) of his Lutheranism. So he joined the Air Force, where he served in Vietnam and then stayed in as a career military man.

Mark, Bob, and I were all strongly religious. We each wanted to do what God called us to do. But we each saw a different way opening. Why was that? Was there one right way and one of us found it, while the other two messed up?

No.

Each way was the right way because we approached it with prayer, study, and a deep desire for God's leading. Each one of us was led by the light we'd been given. What light I had at eighteen came from an evangelical Quaker congregation that was conservative politically and my family with much the same convictions. I could have registered as a conscientious objector, but I didn't have any clear leading either to go to war or to be a conscientious objector. I was led safely into student status.

Bob, on the other hand, was affiliated with a group of Friends that, like many other Quakers, was against the war (any war—not just Vietnam), and was raised with a biblical and social understanding much different from my own. His faith was saturated with calls against the war and for peace.

Lutheran Mark Peterson saw national service as a way to be a Christian. He still feels the same way—that his service in the military was a major part of his living out his faith.

What these three stories show is that we have to be led by the light given to us. We can't be led by another's light; it will be unable to really light our way because we don't own or understand it. Neither Bob's way nor Mark's way could have been my way—I wasn't in a place to own or understand either one. God worked with me in God's time and not the government's, the church's, or my family's.

These stories also show a need to respect others whose ways are not our ways. This respect grows from faith, especially when we have the chance for faithful dialogue with others whose way led them to a place that we ourselves would not go. Listening to each other with spiritual ears wide open helps us to understand each other.

LEADINGS MAY OPEN NEW WAYS

When we listen to others talk about their leadings and how they came to them and obeyed them, we may find a new way opening for ourselves. During the years of the Vietnam Conflict, as I met more young men who were in opposition to the war on religious grounds, I began to question my own stance. I read the Bible and writings by many types of Christians. I moved toward the pro-peace stance that I have today, believing that, as a Christian, I should not participate in war. But this is light that I've been given for my life. This is the leading I followed. This is where my sacred compass led me. As I followed my sacred compass and lived up to the light I was given, I found that God gave me even more and the way became more illumined for me.

As we learn to obey the voice of God within us, guided by our leadings, prayers, worship, Bible reading, and testing our leadings for:

- ♦ beauty
- ♦ caring
- ♦ faith
- ♦ feeling in harmony with God
- ♦ kindness
- ♦ generosity
- ♦ joy
- ♦ patience
- ♦ love
- ♦ gentleness
- ♦ peace

- persistence
- rightness
- surrendering of our wills to God
- self-control

we find the signs of way opening more apparent. True leadings get us ready for action. They take us to new places, new ways of thinking, new ways of acting, new ways of choosing life. They take us to new ways of daring to say, "Speak, Lord, thy servant is listening."

FOUR

TESTING OUR LEADINGS

Seasons of Discernment

I'M FIXIN' TO, commencin' to, plannin' to get ready to start." That's what a fellow I know says when asked how things are going on any project he's working on. The truth is that George is a lot farther down the road when he says that than most people are at the end of a project.

In the same way that George has his fixin' to, commencin' to, plannin' to get ready to start stage, so, too, are there stages in following our sacred compass and checking our leadings against it. These stages are sensing, waiting, and acting. But following our sacred compass is not a rigidly linear process, so you might not approach these stages in the order I list here. Your waiting may lead back to sensing, or forward to action. Likewise, action may lead you back to sensing or waiting. Often, the three are a synthesis of each other—a blend of sensing and waiting while acting, for example. They flow one to another and back around. This nonlinear movement is disconcerting to those like me who crave order and reason, but is the nature of true spiritual work. Yet, naming the stages helps us see where we are in testing our leadings and sensing additional signs, and lets our soul know where we are in the process of following our sacred compass.

SENSING

Sensing Is a Time of Testing

Sensing is when we begin to deeply examine our leadings. This stage is a living laboratory of spiritual experience and experimentation. I don't mean that we need to try out new religions or belief systems, but that this is a time to test the leadings our soul feels.

Sensing Is a Time of Looking

Sensing is also a time to look for God's direction in both ordinary and unexpected ways. The ordinary signs are easy to accept. We expect to uncover God's grace in daily times of quiet prayer or meeting with spiritual friends. After all, when we're in a reflective, care-full time of communion with God, we're naturally more open to the Spirit's moving.

We also need to be open to the Spirit's prompting, inspiring, or confirming a leading in unexpected ways. These may be a trusted friend saying something about a topic that he or she doesn't know we've been thinking about, seeing a newspaper story about the subject on our heart, hearing a song on the radio that speaks to our condition, or a thought coming to us while mowing the lawn.

Sensing Is a Time of Being Wise

We do have to be careful not to read into either the ordinary or the extraordinary meanings that are not present in our time of sensing. We don't want to be like the old-time farmer who prayed for a sign, witnessed the clouds forming the letters *PC*, and so climbed off his tractor and spent the rest of his years as an unsuccessful evangelist who never had even one convert. Upon arriving in heaven, he asked God, "I did what you told me. I saw the *PC* and so left everything to Preach Christ." "No," said God. "It meant 'Plant Corn.'"

Sensing Is a Time of Awareness

Sensing is a time to be open to and aware of the subtle shifts that we would otherwise miss, if not paying careful spiritual attention. I was reminded of this while reading Robert Hellenga's novel *Philosophy Made Simple*. Rudy, the protagonist, was having trouble sleeping one night, so he turned on his radio and listened to a religious broadcast. People called in to the show he listened to and told the hosts about ways that God had given them a sense of direction. The hosts, Bob and Helen, gave every story a theological framework, saying, "God has a plan for each and every one of us. We need to find the plan":

> One man, for example, called in to say that he'd been struck by lightning on the golf course, on a Sunday morning. The lightning had knocked a nine-iron right out of his hands on the fifth hole, but it hadn't harmed him. He never took up his clubs again. Didn't even pick up that club that had been knocked out of his hand. Just left it lying on the

fairway. He went on to become a successful preacher.

Rudy started to roll his eyes in the dark, but then he realized that he was no different from the man with the golf club.

Yes, we need to pay attention to the signs; but we need to make sure they are signs from God and not just a sign of lightning's attraction to a nine-iron. Our time of sensing will not go unrewarded. Jesus reminds us, "Ask, and it will be given you; seek, and you will find; knock, and it will be opened to you." God's direction will be revealed if we spend the sensing time needed to allow it to flower in us.

SENSING LAB EXPERIMENT 1
Where's the Leading Coming From?

Asking yourself this question helps you to see if the leading is driven by your ego or by a prompting from God. Ask yourself if the leading is free from

- ◆ self will
- ◆ self-centeredness
- ◆ self-serving influences
- ◆ undue outside influences

The answer is unlikely to be a "pure" yes. We are rarely completely untainted by self-interest or the promptings and advice from the voices we respect. We're human—"self" is part of who we are. But if a certain leading is driven by your ego, that is a good clue that the leading is not from God.

The opposite is also true. If a leading feels like it's from God and exhibits love, joy, peace, longsuffering, gentleness, goodness, faith, meekness, temperance (those spiritual fruits from the book of Galatians), you can be certain it isn't being driven entirely by ego.

SENSING LAB EXPERIMENT 2

Is the Leading Clear?

Next, look at your thinking about the leading. Is your thinking clear, or is your mind a morass? One way to test clarity of thought is to ask what you're trying to discern. You might ask, "What am I sensing this leading to be?" and then try to answer the question in fifty words or less: *I'm feeling led to pray more* or *I sense I should call a friend and give them a word of encouragement* or *I hear God saying I need to. . . .* You get the idea. If you can't put the leading succinctly into words, it is a sign that you're not clear and that you either need to dismiss the leading or give it room to emerge with more clarity.

SENSING LAB EXPERIMENT 3

Is the Leading Compelling?

When I teach writing workshops, many people ask me what it takes to be a writer. By that, they mean a published writer. They're looking for answers such as talent, training, and a good agent. Instead, I ask them, "Can you *not* write?" I cannot *not* write; I'm compelled to write. Similarly, true leadings will not be dismissed; they are compelling and unshakeable. Setting a leading aside is a way to test its quality and intensity. If it returns clearer and more focused, you can trust your leading more fully.

SENSING LAB EXPERIMENT 4

How Does the Leading Fit Your Life?

Another test is to ask how the leading fits into the rhythm of your life. If you're feeling led to quit your job and live as a monastic, does that fit with your current situation, or does it have something to do with obnoxious coworkers and the screaming kids at home? This is an important question to consider because leadings don't just affect us. In our soulful excitement, we often forget that. Discern how your leading affects those around you—family, congregation, coworkers, and so on. The leading may be yours, but true leadings will not take us completely outside our life's patterns in ways that would do emotional or spiritual violence to the people around us.

SENSING LAB EXPERIMENT 5

Does the Leading Come from God's Love?

True leadings grow out of our love for God and God's love for us and others. If we choose life, then we also choose love. We must be moved by and sensitive to love's moving in us.

Love must be our initial inspiration. Ask yourself if you are led from something other than love for God, love for God's direction, or love for God's people or creation. If so, your leading is amiss. Paying attention to the motions of love is at the heart of following our sacred compass. Following the way of love leads us to become spiritually sensitive women and men, no matter where the leading takes us.

SENSING LAB EXPERIMENT 6
Will the Leading Change You?
While many leadings are about helping others, God also uses our leadings to help us. Our first instinct should not be toward an action to fix something. Rather, a leading rooted in divine love leads us deeper into our life with God. True leadings take us into spiritual instruction. Your leading may help others, but you also need to have a keen sense of how you might grow if you follow it. Ask yourself if you will:

- be deepened
- grow spiritually
- experience compassion

You can add to, or subtract from, this list as you think about how following a particular leading might change you, but be prepared for surprises. Sometimes the change from a leading is not something we expect or does not occur immediately. Allow God's timing to be at work.

What Gets Sifted?

Following our sacred compass is a lifelong lesson in discernment. Sensing is the initial stage of beginning to test a leading—to discern if it's the right one for us. Deborah Gavrin Frangquist says that she loves the underlying meaning of the word *discernment*. She says the Latin *dis* means "apart," and *cernere* means "to sift":

> "Sifting apart" carries my imagination into the kitchen, where I sift and separate all kinds of things. . . . Spiritual discernment—discernment about our work, our human relationships, our relationship with God—requires repeated sifting . . . so that we truly use God's gifts, rather than waiting until we are certain we know what to do.

Sifting describes well the important work that goes on during the sensing stage. This is the time to sift to remove the impurities—to shake out your ego, your needs, your demands, until nothing is left but your love for God and God's will for you.

WAITING

In the same way that sensing is ultimately a stage of sifting, Waiting is a stage of deepening and defining. Waiting adds exterior checks to the serious interior examination we're already doing in the sensing stage. In waiting we invite things and people beyond ourselves to help us confirm our leading, because as reliable as interior motions of love are, we want to make sure we are going God's way. These external sources help us reach a deeper affirmation of our leadings. They bring clarity and can show us that we've misread the leading.

The waiting stage is a good time to think about which spiritual practices and tools you can use to follow your sacred compass. You might:

- study Scripture
- read devotional material
- converse with spiritual friends
- journal
- practice guided meditation
- take personal retreats
- use *lectio divina*
- fast
- pray

This is short list; the possible practices are numerous, and it would be impossible to use them all. They all are worth considering, though. Cull the list for those that will be most helpful and fit best with who you are. You might want to try one or two that are outside of your usual spiritual practices or look like they might make you uncomfortable. A bit of discomfort may be just what you need to stretch your growing spiritual edges.

The goal of these practices is to help you release your cares and concerns as you move toward God. A primary purpose of the waiting stage is to move us away from our natural desire for busy-ness and action to a place of prayer and contemplation, rest and reflection.

Waiting Space

A good way to begin the waiting period is to make a special sacred space in which to pray or meditate. Such a space may be a physical one or it may be a period of time you carve out of your day. Making a physical space can be as simple as setting aside a corner of a bedroom with a comfortable chair, good light, and some reading and writing material. You might find the abstract task of setting aside time harder. Think about where in your day you could find or make space for God in an intentional, seeking way. This time doesn't have to be hours at a stretch—it could be gatherings of minutes throughout the day, or a particular hour each day. What is important is that it is right for you and God. Only you and God can determine what is "enough" time. The only gauge is that your time is long enough for you to still your heart and mind to hear God's voice.

Waiting is not to be rushed. The bigger the leading, the more time it needs. Following our sacred compass is not about instantaneous discernment. It's not about, "An answer has come, so let's move on and get busy." Rather, it's about hearing the voice of God—a voice that is rarely rushed.

Waiting with Scripture

Bible reading, including the practice of *lectio divina*, is useful in the waiting time. By this, I mean doing more than using Scripture as a hokey divination tool. You may have heard the joke about the guy who asked what he was supposed to do with his life, picked up the Bible, flipped through it, and stuck his finger in. His finger landed on Matthew 27:5: "and [Judas] went and hanged himself." Not liking that advice, the man tried again. His finger landed next on Luke 10:37: "Jesus said to him, 'Go and do likewise.'"

What the Bible offers us if we read deeply is real stories of real people seeking for and being sought by God. Their stories are a gift to us. Read them with an eye to both how God works with God's people and to what the story is saying to you. Presbyterian pastor Glen Bell says, "When I listen with great care to the Bible, giving thanks to God for the Word that continues to be living and active, I discover discernment."

Lectio divina can be especially helpful in listening with great care. *Lectio divina* is Latin for "divine reading." It's a structured way of combining prayer and scriptural reading that deepens our communion with God and gives us spiritual insight. There are four steps to *lectio divina*. While the sequence below is recommended, don't worry if the steps mix and mingle and don't follow a direct sequence—you should allow them to weave a tapestry of divine guidance together. Let the Holy Spirit work in and through this experience:

◆ *Lectio:* Read a scriptural passage slowly. Stop whenever you feel drawn toward a word, phrase, or thought.

◆ *Meditatio:* Pondering the passage you've read and ask what you think and feel that it means for you.

◆ *Oratio:* Take time to pray and talk with God about the passage and what you're thinking about it.

◆ *Contemplatio:* Rest in God. Still your soul in silence, and say yes to God's love and direction.

Lectio divina invites us to study, ponder, listen, and pray from God's written word to us.

Waiting with the Saints, Old and New

While our leadings are unique to us, we are not the first to follow the sacred compass. Many other faithful people have walked the pilgrim path before us, and some of them have left markers and maps for us in the form of spiritual exercises. The waiting stage is also a good time to practice such spiritual exercises. St. Ignatius's *Spiritual Exercises* can be an especially helpful set of exercises. Another spiritual tool is *Always We Begin Again: The Benedictine Way of Living,* by John McQuiston II, a distillation of the Benedictine Rule for laypersons. McQuiston suggests specific times for meditation throughout the day. His is a book to savor slowly, thoughtfully, and honestly. Phyllis Tickle's books on "praying the hours" also provide helpful reading and guide us into an ancient spiritual practice that is new to many Christians.

Another useful spiritual exercise is guided meditation. Guided meditation involves allowing someone to help you visualize yourself in a spiritual or biblical setting. Guided meditations are often dynamic; for example, you might progress from one place to another in a biblical story, or ask a question and listen for a specific answer. To use guided meditation:

- Sit down and find a comfortable posture.
- Close your eyes, to help you resist distractions.
- Breathe in slowly and invite God to join you. Then exhale slowly while telling God, "I'm here and ready to listen."
- As you hear the guided meditation, use your imagination enter the Scripture story.
- Listen to your feelings and pay attention to your thoughts. Ask yourself what God may want to say to you. What does God want you to do because of what you're hearing?
- Pray and ask God's Spirit to lead you into God's truth.

After doing a guided meditation, you might want to spend some time journaling or sharing your experience with some spiritual friends.

If guided meditation seems like something you'd like to try, I suggest reading Dave Ambrose's *Chew On This: 30 Biblical Devotions into the Heart of Christ*. Though it's written primarily for young adults, the book is an excellent introduction to guided meditation and offers a month's supply of meditations (along with an audio CD of the meditations).

The examen, or examination of conscience, an ancient spiritual practice, helps us pay attention to our nearness to or distance from God. Despite its similarity to the word *examination,* examen is intended to encourage us, not grade us. It helps us recognize God's guidance. It's not about rating our spiritual depth—or lack of it. The examen is usually prayed toward the end of the day and consists of five steps that vary slightly depending upon the teacher. The examen I find most helpful progresses this way: celebration and thanksgiving, asking for illumination, examining the day's events, going through the joys, sorrows, and other emotions of the day, and telling God what grace and power you need. If you need help starting, you can use the following phrases, and add to them:

- I thank you, God, for . . .
- God, you were with me today. What did you see that you want me to pay attention to?
- Help me review my day honestly and well.
- Loving God, help me feel anew the emotions of this day. What are they teaching me?
- Be with me God. Grant me the graces I need to . . .

The exercises of Ignatius and McQuiston, praying the hours, and the prayer of examen offer helpful ways to light the path of discernment. Countless people have used these tools and others over the years to help them clarify God's direction in their lives. Still, not every exercise is for everyone. Mary Cartledgehayes, author of *Grace: A Memoir* and *Semisweetness and Light*, says, "I used the Ignatian exercises in divinity school as part of a spiritual discernment class. It was painful, probably because I'm ADHD and stillness is not the path that brings me closer to God."

If one spiritual exercise doesn't work for you, ask for discernment about continuing to use it. Pray; if you feel released, move on. Regardless of what you use as regular spiritual exercises, you can find benefits in all of them—especially as you try to see God at work in your life and our life at work with God.

Waiting with the Arts

DEVOTIONAL READING I like to enter the waiting period with devotional readings. Some that I use consistently are geared for daily use—Cindy Crosby and Thomas Oden's *Ancient Christian Devotional*, for example. This devotional guide combines excerpts from the writings of the church fathers for either daily or weekly reading and prayer. It follows liturgical cycle A of the *Revised Common Lectionary*. Though, as a non-liturgical Quaker-type, *cycle* for me usually is found on the Maytag and has the words *wash*, *spin*, or *rinse* associated with it, this book puts me in touch with a collective wisdom that

I could miss since it's outside my tradition. Other books that tap into the wealth of Christian devotional writing include Richard Foster's *Devotional Classics* and *Spiritual Classics*, Phyllis Tickle's *The Divine Hours* series, and *Nearer to the Heart of God* by Bernard Bangley.

I also use devotional literature rooted in my tradition—Thomas Kelly's *Testament of Devotion*, George Fox's *Journal*, and *Quaker Faith and Practice*. In these books, I have a connection with people who speak the same spiritual language that I do. You'll want to do the same—seek out the richness of your faith tradition. Pat Cornwell, a Catholic writer friend of mine, says that she uncovers deep spiritual lessons in the "writings of Thomas à Kempis, Thomas Merton, The Rule of St. Benedict, and the writings of Father Thomas Keating, who teaches what is called centering prayer (a form of meditation)."

She continues to explain her "waiting practice" by saying, "The first hour each morning is reserved for such reading (along with the first cup of coffee), followed by time for thanksgiving and listening for the 'small still voice.'" Pat has discovered that there's deep spiritual wisdom closer to our spiritual homes than we often think. The waiting stage is part of exploring that.

READING DEEP As we read devotional literature, we must practice deep reading. By that, I mean reading below the surface. I don't mean looking for hidden meanings; I do mean looking beyond the words to what the words mean for you.

◆ What do the words say to you that is helpful?
◆ What do they say that challenges you?
◆ Does your reading confirm your leading?
    Does it point to a different way?

READING WIDELY Some of my devotional reading comes from untraditional places, especially the fiction shelf. Like many of my friends, I find that any reading is a spiritual discipline when my inner eye is tuned to God. Jo Morgan, one of my oldest friends, says, "It's very difficult for me to read anything without discerning spiritual messages, even if the material was not designed to be particularly spiritual. I'll be reading along and a phrase on the page will pop out at me. I may get chills or have another physical sensation as I recognize the Divine Truth in the author's voice."

You've already seen how *A Prayer for Owen Meany* has influenced my thinking about seeing our lives as God-purposed. Poetry has also been useful to me. I keep a file folder filled with poems in my desk drawers at work and home. Some of the poetry is religious; most isn't. Still, it all speaks to me in ways that even the poet may not be aware of or have contemplated.

VISUAL ARTS Visual arts also come into play for me, which is not surprising, since I was an art major in college. One tool I use to engage the visual arts on a spiritual level is Sylvia Shaw Judson's *The Quiet Eye: A Way of Looking at Pictures*. It's a tiny book of art reproductions accompanied by quotations from William Blake, Martin Buber, van Gogh, and many others. Judson, a sculptor best known for her *Bird Girl* sculpture in Savannah, Georgia, assembled them. Judson wrote the book to be an experience in soulful thought and reflection filled with examples of "divine ordinariness." As such, Judson's book leads me into contemplation of great art and the divine.

MUSIC Deep listening to music is also a form of letting God communicate within while without us. You may use classical pieces by Handel or blues by Handy. Look for music that leads you to the places you need to go—whether high energy or deeply contemplative. An artist named Marcella Beatty is part of a nonprofit community outreach dance troupe that combines praise music with movement, including American Sign Language and classical ballet. She uses "movement as a tool to invite the Holy Spirit to 'dance' within me." Do you need music or lyrics or both?

Waiting with Words

Committing an act of literature is also a good spiritual exercise for the waiting stage. I talked earlier about writing spiritual essays or autobiographies. Here I'm talking about other types of writing, including journaling, creative writing, or letter writing.

Journals have a long history in Christian faith development, describing as they do the writer's spiritual progress—or digress, if the journal writer is honest. Quaker men and women have been writing journals since our movement's earliest days. Many of these are still in print and read by Friends and non-Friends alike. Your tradition may have journals of its own.

A journal is more of a spiritual diary than an explanation of spiritual truth. Journals tend to be the writings of everyday people of faith, which is why they are a good place for us to start. A spiritual journal differs from a diary in the sense that it is not necessarily a record of a day's events. Rather, it's a spiritual reflection on life's journey and a way to be open to God's direction. Communications specialist Jane Mastin says, "[Journal] writing is a peaceful release for me. I enjoy seeing my words on paper just as a way to relax and be open to new ideas, thoughts and the guiding Spirit."

Blogger Ann Kroeker's experience is similar: "Journaling has been a big part of my interaction with the Lord. There, I explore what I think He's telling me, pour out my heart, copy out verses to consider more deeply, write without stopping, freewriting as prayer. This often points me in the direction I need to go or clarifies what I'm concerned about." And denominational executive Ian Evison says, "I have often used journaling. I just write to unroll the depth of what is inside. This stirs other thoughts, dreams, etc."

As with other spiritual practices, you'll need to develop a journaling method that works for you. You may want to buy a journal with a fine cover and quality paper from a bookstore.

Or you might like writing in a spiral binder. You might write with a fountain pen or find typing into a computer file best fits you. The only essential is to be regular about writing. You probably won't find journaling helpful as a spiritual practice if you only write occasionally because this kind of writing, says poet Mary Brown, is "not only a way of expressing, but a way of knowing." Knowing—and seeing what we know—takes the discipline of constancy. A journal written in fits and starts probably won't do you much good. It won't have enough consistency to show anything deep.

Staying in touch with this way of knowing is one reason many journal writers date their entries. It reminds them to be regular, and the dates let them look over the paths they've trod. Writer Lois Jordan does that. That way, she says, "As I look back on what I have written, I am sometimes surprised at what I find—as though my hand were guided. I find journaling one of my most helpful discernment tools."

You might want to begin journaling with a brief opening about what's going on in your life, to place your writing and insight in a specific place and time. Write what comes to mind. You might include:

- Bible verses
- spiritual wisdom that has special meaning for you
- thoughts from practicing *lectio divina* or the examen
- insight from your devotional reading

◆ prayers that you've offered—and answers you've received
◆ new awareness of God in your life
◆ feelings—joy, sorrow, elation, calmness

Nothing is too deep or shallow for your journal—epiphanies whether while reading the Bible or taking a walk around the block are equally valid.

Above all, don't edit your writing. Allow it to flow. Don't worry about correctness. Try your hand at poetry or storytelling if you feel so called. Remember, Jesus often taught in stories. We tend to call them by the more holy-sounding title of "parables," but they were stories for spiritual enlightenment. What stories could you write? What poems come to mind? You're not writing for posterity—you're writing for your own spiritual learning. Other forms of writing as spiritual discernment include letter writing, blogging, poetry, prayers, and musings.

Use whatever forms appeal to you—things that help you confirm your leadings and show you the way the sacred compass is pointing.

Waiting with Friends

Spiritual friendship is a friendship between people committed to each other and to the deepening of their faith lives. Margaret Guenther says the characteristics of spiritual friendship include "a gift of hospitality, presence and dialogue" given to another. Mike Kinder, a businessman, has been meeting with the same group for fourteen years. Mike says, "These friendships allow me the opportunity to voice my questions and concerns to people who listen without judgment and offer their own thoughts and beliefs." Glen Bell, a clergyman, also finds spiritual friends helpful. Glen says his weekly meeting

> for conversation, worship and prayer with two excellent friends has frequently been a great blessing to me. They know me, warts and all. They love me, amid my strengths, convictions, failings, gifts and blind spots. They often know just the right thing to say, to query, to suggest, even if it be painfully revealing in the moment.

In addition to giving gifts of hospitality, presence, and dialogue, spiritual friendships also offer the gift of safety, because these friendships are built on trust and spiritual growth. In them, our souls still. That stillness invites our friends to rest inside the safety of spiritual community and trust.

Waiting with Our Bodies

The waiting time is also a time to practice sensual spirituality—tasting, feeling, and sensing God in the world around us. While we often think of discernment as soul work, God created our bodies. They are teachers and conductors of God's wisdom to us.

I was reminded of that when two of my friends, Barry and Allan, were teasing me about the books I've written, calling them my "Quaker sound and sights books." They challenged me to write one on smell. While we laughed about that, at a deeper level it struck me how little we use our senses to experience God. And yet the Bible is full of verses or examples urging us to do just that. Take Psalm 34:8, a verse that tells us to "taste and see that the LORD is good," This is more than just a spiritual metaphor. If it is indeed God who made us, then God made us body and soul. The evidence for experiencing God through our bodies is abundant in Scripture.

A simple way to experience sensual spirituality is to use the following exercise. Take a piece of paper and write these phrases down the left-hand side:

- ◆ Smells like
- ◆ Tastes like
- ◆ Sounds like
- ◆ Feels likes
- ◆ Looks like

Now, take a spiritual concept such as discernment or holiness and put that word in front of each of those phrases. Then complete the phrase. What does holiness smell like, taste like, sound like, feel like, and look like? How does this sensual spirituality open you to experiencing God's leading in a new way?

Waiting with Whatever Works

There are as many ways to practice discernment as there are people. God comes to us in the places we stand through the things we do. The ways vary, as do God's people. That's what I found when I surveyed people I knew about this topic. One woman said that "fasting in conjunction with prayer has often been the circumstance in which God has given me insight, leading, or discernment." Another said, "Service. In serving others, much is revealed. I'm kind of lazy and God unearths a lot . . . when I finally serve people."

Other friends talked about how running, biking, and hiking helped open their minds and hearts for long stretches of time, allowing them to think prayerfully about what God was saying to them. Max Carter, a campus minister in North Carolina, reported, "I find that when I go for long runs or other focused physical exercise before I have to give a talk or make a major decision, I have serious openings and insights that are gifts to me. It goes deeper than just 'clearing the mind.' "

Others wrote to me about walking a labyrinth—and one suggested that this was especially helpful for people who learn best by moving their bodies and stimulating their muscles as they learn. Some suggested sitting still in a beautiful church, while others were helped by reflecting on the meaning of their dreams.

Some respondents talked about working in their gardens or walking on a beach. One said that outdoor time was a helpful spiritual exercise because "nature is the best setting for spiritual growth. We know that God is present everywhere, but where are we? We are usually not present to God. In the natural world, we get a clue to the magnificence of God, and the awe this inspires goes a long way to help us listen." Others talked about how revelations seemed to come up while doing routine things, such as showering, driving, cooking, or cleaning. One added, "Especially vacuuming, which I despise."

I think singer-songwriter Carrie Newcomer summed it up best when she said, "Essentially, a life well lived is a spiritual exercise." Indeed.

All of the things we do in the waiting time feed our souls. As our souls are nourished, we find discerning God's voice easier. Time, along with our souls, slows. The direction needle stills and surely points the direction. The leading becomes clear. We increase our strength to move farther along the pilgrim path.

ACTION

The final stage is action. Here, we move out in faith into a new ministry, new job, new life situation, or to wherever we are called. In this phase, we begin to actively follow our leadings.

As we move into action, we find ourselves fully engaged in the art of living—a deep way of living that transforms us in powerful and sometimes subtle ways. That's because, as Horace B. Pointing wrote:

The art of living must be studied, as must every art. It calls for imagination, so that every advance, every change, is not merely a difference, but a creative act. Achievement, at any level above the lowest, calls for courage to hold on, in spite of current moods, and for exacting self-discipline. The art of Christian living calls for the same self-preparation; but its reward is not merely aesthetic satisfactions. The soul, hungry for God, is fed. Life itself takes on new meaning. Thus it is that we break from the confines of the prisons we have built about ourselves. Thus it is we are brought into the freedom of the Kingdom of God which, every day, through the wide world, is being realised in the hearts of men.

As I said, this process is not absolutely linear. Just because this is the action stage, doesn't mean that you're not continuing to do things from the previous two stages. You should continue with journaling, doing *lectio divina*, reading the Bible, and any number of things that you did earlier. Continue to check your leading as you progress—to see if way continues to be open or suddenly closes. Pay attention. Does your acting include compassion, charity, generosity, forgiveness, healing, and spiritual empowerment?

Check what is going on around you as you act out your leading. Do you come upon unexpected twists and turns? If so, ask yourself if that twist is a sign to slow down, or if this turn says, "Check your compass." Do you need to take some sensing time or some time to work on some of the waiting activities?

The advantage of the steps within the steps—

- ◆ such as Sensing and its checking the leading against love
- ◆ or Waiting and its waiting with the saints

—is that they are things that we can do as we move through acting. As we develop spiritual practices that feed our souls, we find ourselves better able to act with humility, confidence, and power, since we know God guides us. God uses sensing, waiting, and acting as constant processes to assure us of our leadings. The steps keep our souls focused on the sacred compass, and our feet on the pilgrim path.

FIVE

THE DARK PATH

What If You Lose Your Way?

S EVERAL YEARS AGO, my friend Maura attended an urban ministry conference at Old First Presbyterian Church in San Francisco. After an evening session, Maura arrived at the hotel and realized she'd left her purse on the sanctuary floor eight blocks away. Her hotel room key sat safely inside her purse. As she turned back to the church, one conference attendee offered to walk back in the dark with her. He was an extremely hard-of-hearing older man, so conversation was minimal.

When Maura and her new friend arrived at the church, they found the front doors locked, so they went around the block to the back of the church. The basement door was unlocked. In they went. Her friend decided to wait in the basement while she ran up to the sanctuary to retrieve her purse.

She entered the empty church and quickly found her purse, but when she tried to leave through the same door she'd entered by, she couldn't. It had locked behind her. She thought about screaming at the top of her lungs, but knew her helpful hard-of-hearing friend wouldn't hear her. After thinking awhile, she decided to try to exit at the back of the sanctuary through the foyer, and then out to the street. She went through two sets of glass doors into the foyer. Success. When she got to the church's wooden doors, though, she found them locked. There was nothing to do but to retrace her steps. When she got to the glass doors, she discovered that they had locked behind her. Now she was trapped in a small section of the church's foyer, engulfed in darkness, surrounded by locked doors.

She sat down on the floor and thought through her options. If worse turned to worst, which it seemed to be doing, she would have to spend the night in the foyer. She decided to make one last attempt to escape the church. She felt along the floor until she touched the old wooden doors that led to the street. She worked her hands up the doors, searching for locks and latches. She tried every knob and latch, but none budged. Finally, she pushed against the door with all her might. The next thing she knew, she had tumbled out the door and was lying on the sidewalk next to a snoozing homeless fellow. Shaking herself off, she found her friend waiting at the basement door, and they made their way back to the hotel.

◆

There are times while following the sacred compass that we feel as if we're locked in a dark church, unable, like Maura, to find our way in or out even from a site of spirituality. The standstill we come to is not for lack of trying, but we still find ourselves in a stuckness of the worse possible sort. We're not stuck because we just plopped down in the middle of the way and gave up, but because we were trying to follow our sacred compass and the path it led us on turned into muck. So, what went wrong?

Following God shouldn't be this hard, should it? Our instincts tell us that if we desire God's will, the path should be easier than this. But our instincts also tell us that the path to God is hard and we're lost. Something in our soul asks, *So, is this the way?* Other questions quickly flood in:

- *How did I get lost?*
- *Am I really lost?*
- *Is this lostness part of the way?*
- *What pocket is that sacred compass in?!*

LOSTNESS MAY BE PART OF OUR WAY

Maura found that the feeling of lostness was part of her way. She discovered that it helped her in ways she could only find by being lost. As she reflected on her time in the locked church, she saw that this dark time mirrored challenges in her life. At the same time she was lost in church, Maura was struggling with decisions and choices that seemed to lead to nowhere or to disaster. "Each successive decision had cut me off from other good options," she said. She also remembered a sermon she'd heard about Jesus and the two disciples on the Emmaus road.

The Emmaus story recalls how, on the day of the Resurrection, the original Easter Sunday, two of the disciples were walking the seven miles from Jerusalem to the town of Emmaus. While on their way, they talked about the brutal events of recent days. As they walked and talked, the risen Jesus joined them.

Hearing their discussion, Jesus asked what events they were discussing. The disciple Cleopas answered Jesus' question with a question: "Are you the only visitor to Jerusalem who does not know the things that have happened there in these days?" Then Jesus began to speak to them, illuminating the scriptures from Moses and the prophets onward, using them to point to the passion and resurrection. They were amazed at his knowledge, but didn't recognize Jesus. As mealtime approached, the two disciples invited Jesus to eat with them. It was only as he broke bread for their meal that they knew who Jesus was. At the breaking of the bread, Jesus vanished from their sight. They jumped up and headed back to Jerusalem, where the other disciples and word of the Resurrection awaited them.

Maura says she remembered that sermon because the preacher pointed out that the two disciples were walking away from Jerusalem. They were going the wrong direction, heading away from Good News. That was when Jesus appeared to them. "I then heard the comforting words, 'Even though you've been going in the wrong direction, I am with you,'" Maura said. "I resolved to pay attention to where God was leading me. I no longer believed that past decisions forever closed off the possibility of joy in my life. God would still lead me back to Jerusalem."

It wasn't as if the sun broke through. Everything wasn't cheery and bright after that. No, the larger context of Maura's being locked in the church was that it happened at a time she was receiving pastoral counseling. For two years, she'd been dealing with a crucial life decision. She'd explored every possible strategy and nothing made a difference. The experience of the dark, locked church led her to a new place. "After being locked up in the church," she says, "I told the counselor the following week that I [made a decision]. My life began again."

Maura's story illustrates how being "lost" or "going the wrong way" may in fact be the right way for a particular time.

LOSTNESS IS HARD AND GOOD

While lostness may be the right way at the right time, that doesn't make it easy. But lostness as a part of the spiritual journey fits with the idea that our lives are pilgrimages. They are pilgrimages to God. We soon discover that pilgrimages are rarely journeys of ease or comfort.

The pilgrimage of Camino de Santiago is an example of this type of journey. Also known as the Way of St. James, the Camino de Santiago has existed for over a thousand years. Upward of ten thousand Christian pilgrims journey the Camino de Santiago annually. The religious travelers following it make their way to Santiago de Compostela, where legend holds that St. James's remains are buried.

There is no single route for the Camino de Santiago; the spiritual explorer chooses from a number of pilgrimage paths. What each shares in common with the other routes is that they all cover five hundred miles and take about a month or more to traverse. The most popular route is the French Way. It comes across the rugged Pyrenees at Roncesvalles in northern Spain and moves down into to the more temperate climes of the valleys of Navarre and La Rioja. From there, the French Way moves through the Castilian plains before climbing again into the hills of Galicia. Along the way, pilgrims stay at inns, hostels, and retreat sites in exchange for a small donation.

Mennonite minister and professor Arthur Paul Boers traveled the Camino de Santiago. When people asked him about his pilgrimage he usually summed up the trip by saying, "It was very hard and incredibly good."

Indeed as I read and re-read my journal of that trip, I seldom see any day that was simply easy. And sometimes more than one day felt like the hardest so far! But all of them without exception also had unexpected blessings and compensations.

That's because pilgrimage "unites belief with action, thinking with doing" and requires that "the body and its actions express the desires and beliefs of the soul."

Arthur's experience of hardship along the pilgrim path— whether outer or inner—is not unique. As Parker Palmer says, "In the tradition of pilgrimage, those hardships are seen not as accidental but as integral to the journey itself. Treacherous terrain, bad weather, taking a fall, getting lost—challenges of that sort, largely beyond our control, can strip the ego of the illusion that it is in charge and make space for the true self to emerge."

Questions that arise when we feel lost along are a good thing, as is discomfort. Discomfort directs us to ask the important questions:

- Have you read your sacred compass correctly?
- Are you here by mistake?
- Did you come to this place on your own, or is God with you?
- What is God saying to you through this way?

Sometimes we may seem to be on the wrong road. Sometimes it *is* the wrong road. But that's okay, for, as St. Paul reminds us, "We know that all things work together for good for those who love God, to those who are called according to his purpose." And that includes wrong roads, and feeling lost.

LOSTNESS FEELS LIKE SPIRITUAL CRISIS

There's been much written recently about Mother Teresa's presumed crisis of faith. After a particularly intense encounter with God, the lines of communication between Mother Teresa and God seemed to go dead. She told her spiritual director that within her heart, "The silence and the emptiness is so great that I look and do not see, listen and do not hear." In 1955 she wrote, "The more I want Him, the less I am wanted. . . . Such deep longing for God—and . . . repulsed—empty—no faith—no love—no zeal." In a letter addressed to Jesus, she pleads, "Lord, my God, who am I that You should forsake me? . . . If there be a God—please forgive me . . . I am told that God loves me, and yet the reality of darkness and coldness and emptiness is so great that nothing touches my soul."

These words certainly sound like the anguished cries of someone losing her spiritual way. And yet, Mother Teresa stayed on her holy path, the path on which her vivid experience set her. For all her soul's wavering, her service stayed steadfast.

It is a sometimes-disconcerting reality of the spiritual life that a devout Christian may harbor insecurity and distress for years. Many Christians know Mother Teresa's heart-struggle well. St. John of the Cross, in his classic *Dark Night of the Soul,* says that the way to sublime and total union with God comes only after trials filled with deep spiritual suffering and feelings of abandonment. While many of us never pass through such a dark spiritual night, we recognize the fact that few of us, no matter how faithful, experience God joyfully on a constant basis. We sense the call to God and the life of the spirit. The separation between our day-to-day life and the realm of the eternal is something that feels too large to completely bridge. And so we settle for a glimpse of the divine.

Could it be, and I wonder if this is true for Mother Teresa, that some encounters with God are so powerful, so life changing and rearranging, that every other experience from that time forward pales in its light? Could the darkness Mother Teresa felt be the darkness that comes after staring into the brightness of the noonday sun? Catherine Phillips, an Episcopal priest, helped me gain this understanding through her poem, "Mother Theresa":

Now that Mother Theresa
Is in the Palpable Presence of God
Held
Fully Held
In the Light she couldn't comprehend
For so many years
Now that she Knows
She is Beloved

What of the years held in The Dark
The years of letter after letter
Eloquent heart-wrenching

letter after letter?
Words she didn't ever want shared
With the world
now published for all to see
Sure to be a best seller
Now that Mother Theresa
Knows herself loved and cherished
Does she want her letters published?
Does she care?
And
Is she willing to join the brighter ring of saints?
Will she do the required three miracles
Or maybe just do one or two for now
Make 'em wait and watch
(And maybe think a bit about publishing those letters)
Is she laughing now
Full-throated gut-busting
Laughter
I like to picture her
Laughing

Mother Teresa's experience, while unique to her, is not unknown to other pilgrims. St. Ignatius tells us that when he began to follow the holy path, he experienced great swings in his soul's condition. There were times he was so distraught that praying or attending Mass didn't help. At other times, the Mass nourished his soul and his prayer life took him to heaven. He was bothered by these shifts, and said to himself, "What new life is this that we are now beginning?"

We may feel the same way, as if we are adrift on a sea of spiritual emotions, lost between agony and ecstasy. The time of feeling lost and being in a place of uncertainty is a dwelling place that will change us, if we allow it. Writer Kate Young Caley says this:

Life is a journey with many turns: we turn toward God, away from God. Then back to God once more. Over and over. We loop and circle and seek, toward new ways of understanding the complexities of life and faith.

Our feeling lost helps us to turn toward God in prayer even as we feel turned away in spirit. It helps us to look at the Bible and devotional writing over and over. To loop into journal writing and circle our spiritual friends and then seek solace from the Holy Spirit. To use and reuse the very tools that we used to confirm our leading. And then to trust them and God.

LOSTNESS MAY BE NOT OF OUR OWN MAKING

While we want to control our life's path, we don't always have that choice. For all of our desire to follow the sacred compass, something outside of us may force us onto a path not of our choosing. That was true for Etty Hillesum, who was sent to Auschwitz by the Nazis. Cleary, this was not a trip of her choosing. Hillesum kept a diary while at Auschwitz, until she died at age twenty-nine. What is remarkable about Hillesum's diary is that it reveals her sense of God's presence in this literal hellhole. Her diary also shows how she used being there as a path to God. She didn't have the three score and ten years the psalmist says are allotted for our lives. She lived decades in days, and her diary shows the spiritual maturation of her life packed into just two years. By the end of her diary, Etty was a different woman from the one who began the journal, writing, "Oh God, take me in your big hand and make me your instrument, let me write for you."

Few of us would consider a concentration camp a place for ecstatic experiences of the divine. It would seem to be the most lost of lost places—a place where the holy path would be impossible to find no matter how sincerely one looked.

Yet, Hillesum saw God at Auschwitz. "Sometimes when I stand in some corner of the camp, my feet planted on Your earth, my eyes raised towards Your heaven, tears sometimes run down my face, tears of deep emotion and gratitude."

Hillesum was not in denial. She acknowledged the horror of the Holocaust and realized that her "lostness" was not because of any failing of hers. Others had thrust her into a place where she could surrender to lostness—or look for the sacred compass even in the midst of that human-caused awfulness. She chose the latter. She wrote, "And I want to be there right in the thick of what people call horror and still be able to say: life is beautiful. Yes, I lie here in a corner, parched and dizzy and feverish and unable to do a thing. Yet I am also with the jasmine and the piece of sky beyond my window."

When we feel lost, it might be time to check the compass. It might be an opportunity for a realistic assessment of the situation and what, if anything, we can do about it:

- Ask yourself how you got in the situation. Answer honestly.
- Did you get there on your own?
- If so, can you go back the way you came or undo what is done?
- Ask if you even want to go back.
- If where you are is caused by others, is there anything you can do about it—other than control your response?
- Can you pray for forgiveness for them?
- Can you accept that you have no control?
- Can you trust God?
- Can you learn something?

Hillesum's diary chronicles her dialogue with God. She wrote, "For once you have begun to walk with God, you need only keep on walking with God and all of life becomes one long stroll—a marvelous feeling."

While the Nazis chose that Hillesum's pilgrimage would lead to physical death, she refused to be bowed by the lostness and, if not quite embracing it, used it as a way to continue pointing her to God. Not many of us may be able to do that as well as Hillesum did. But she shows us how, by endeavoring to faithfully follow the sacred compass even when lostness is imposed upon us, walking with God can ultimately be "a marvelous feeling."

LOSTNESS CAN LEAD TO HOPE

While Hillesum's lostness was imposed upon her and led to her death, sometimes our lostness, as we pay attention to it, leads to healing. That was true for a member of a book club I co-lead. She told me about how she suffered from depression off and on for most of her life. It took her some time to comprehend the depth of her difficulty because she always seemed to pull herself together after each bout of depression, and so attributed her depression to particular stressors or circumstances. But during her first pregnancy and the birth of her daughter, she says

the bottom dropped out. My being and my soul crackled, shredded, and broke into a zillion pieces. I was a robot who could barely get through the day. I then knew I had to receive treatment, but didn't know how to go about it. God led me to my ob/gyn who referred me to his wife's psychiatrist. . . . Somehow I knew God wanted me to see this psychiatrist. After a year or so of medical treatment, [my doctor referred me to another doctor] for "talk therapy." I always felt that God wanted me to keep going back for treatment and work with the doctors—no matter how dreadful the work was. God was with me throughout the treatment—hospitalizations and all. God worked through these doctors to help me recover to the point that I can now live a normal life—work, volunteer, play, and enjoy a great relationship with my children and many friends.

As horrid a path as it was to travel, my friend's was a path of ultimate health because of some choices she made. In her lostness, she:

- admitted she needed help
- accepted advice, even hard advice
- followed doctor's orders
- allowed others to help her

Our lives may have parallels to hers, or they may be completely different. Still, we choose how we respond, in fear or in trust. Noel Paul Stookey sings in one of his songs, "There's a reason for living down in the valleys, that only the mountains know." The mountains' understanding is one we may not achieve in this lifetime, but God has promised our ultimate safekeeping and a wisdom that will be fully ours in the light of eternity.

LOSTNESS—IT'S NOT ALWAYS ABOUT US

There's another kind of lostness, too. That is the lostness of wondering, after acting on a leading, whether we heard the leading correctly—or incorrectly. Sitting in Starbucks a while ago, a writing student of mine and I were talking about leadings and the joy and trepidation of following them. Katherine told me about a leading she had to go to Alaska and do some grant-writing for a community there.

It was a leading that took Katherine fifteen months to become clear about. Part of her clearness came through the persistence of the leading. God used quirky ways to get through to her. One was on the day she had to make the final decision about whether to go to Alaska or not. Sitting at a stoplight in front of her was an old pickup with a camper and a solitary bumper sticker proclaiming, "See You In Alaska." That sealed the deal. She ended up going to Alaska.

"This was so big in my life," she said, "that I was certain that my life would be radically changed. I would be a different person. Changed in amazing ways. But I wasn't. I came home and was the same old me."

So we talked over coffee about whether that leading was a real one or not. Shouldn't there have been some major spiritual outcome from following a leading that took that long to become clear? She said she began to wonder whether the leading was true or not. Though she didn't label it as such, I saw her wondering as an expression of lostness. Did she misread a sign? Take the wrong trail?

As we talked more, she mentioned how she took her daughter, sons, and niece with her to Alaska. The experience radically changed their lives—they moved from self-involved teens to socially active and aware young adults in the workplace and graduate school. So what does that say about leadings? Do they always have to radically change us? Maybe they change those walking along the way with the led. And it may be only given to us much later that our being lost was someone's else path to being found.

TO BE LOST IS NOT TO BE DAMNED

In the New Testament, the word *lost* means simply that, "lost." It doesn't mean being doomed or damned for all eternity. It means that whatever is lost is in the wrong place; it's not where it should be. This is true in all of Jesus' parables (such as the one about the lost coin) and about people, too. Things and people are lost when they are not in the right place.

How many times on a road trip have you been traveling along, enjoying the scenery, or shouting encouragement to slower drivers, and missed a turn-off or taken a wrong road? We've all experienced times while traveling that we found ourselves where we shouldn't be—sometimes even heading the opposite direction completely. It's like the pilot who's hopelessly lost in the fog. He comes on the intercom and tells his passengers, "I've got some good news and some bad news. The bad news is, I don't have a clue where we are. The good news is we're making great time." That's how it is with us sometimes, in travel and in life. We're uncertain where we are, but we know we're making great time. That's okay. As novelist Doris Bett's said, "Faith is not synonymous with certainty . . . [but] is the decision to keep your eyes open." Keeping our eyes open helps lead us out of the lostness and to our right place—with God.

LOSTNESS SAYS, "CHECK THE COMPASS"

Feeling lost also reminds us that we get that way sometimes because we didn't keep our eyes open and watch the signs. As the words of the prayer of general confession from *The Book of Common Prayer* read:

Almighty and most merciful Father; We have erred and strayed from thy ways like lost sheep. We have followed too much the devices and desires of our own hearts. We have offended against thy holy laws. We have left undone those things which we ought to have done; And we have done those things which we ought not to have done; and there is no health in us. But thou, O Lord, have mercy upon us, miserable offenders. Spare thou those, O God, who confess their faults. Restore thou those who are penitent;

According to thy promises declared unto mankind In Christ Jesus our Lord. And grant, O most merciful Father, for his sake; That we may hereafter live a godly, righteous and sober life, To the glory of thy holy Name. Amen.

Leadings give us a reason to question whether or not we're lost. We need a faith that questions us as we question it. We need to remember that we have not arrived, but are still on the trail. Difficult times help us focus on the fact that there are areas in our lives in which we still need to grow.

In the words of the King James Version of the Bible, the psalmist cries out, "Search me, O God, and know my heart: try me, and know my thoughts: And see if there be any wicked way in me, and lead me in the way everlasting." One point of following the sacred compass is to be led into God's presence and have our hearts searched, to be led in the life everlasting. This is a need as old as the human search for God and God's search for us.

Lostness also shows us that leadings may not be for all time. "There can be times in our lives when an utterly logical course, which was previously satisfying, suddenly seems barren or false— or it may just close down, forcing us into painful re-examination of the way we are to go," says Patricia Loring. As our life's circumstances change, we may find our way changing, too. In fact, we should expect life to change. And whether such changes are minor or massive, they can cause a feeling of lostness.

I thought I was on the way, but . . . is an unsettling feeling. Instead of focusing on the feeling of lostness, you might look at your call to commitment. Are you being faithful? Are you checking your compass? If, after some soul examination, you answer "yes," then move ahead. Perhaps you're just between trails. You're still committed to the pilgrimage, but now are picking your way through the dense underbrush of a massive forest blocking out the light.

Miraculous things happen when we start clearing our way literally and figuratively. Writer Mary Cartledgehayes says, "Chopping brush is one of the most effective [spiritual] tools for me. In the process of making a clear physical space in which the air can move more freely, I find clarity in the spiritual spaces as well." We clear space, check the compass, and trust God.

When we are committed to following the sacred compass, God honors our commitment.

LOSTNESS TEACHES THROUGH CLOSINGS

Remember my friend Maura, who was locked inside the church? She also found that closed doors behind her taught her as much as open doors ahead. "There is as much guidance in what closes behind us as there is in way that opens ahead of us. The opening may reveal our potentials while the closing may reveal our limits—two sides of the same coin," says Parker Palmer. Our hearts, when we take stock of our lives, tell us that is true. For many of God's pilgrims, way closing behind has had the same type of guiding effect as way opening before.

That was true for Thomas Kelly, one of my favorite spiritual writers. His *Testament of Devotion*, considered a spiritual classic, hasn't been out of print since its initial publication in 1944, but Kelly's coming to write this powerful little book was the result of doors closing. He hoped for a career as an academic and missionary to Japan. He first studied chemistry, and then went to seminary to prepare for his work in Japan. Instead, he was called to teach Bible at a college in Ohio. He went back to seminary to work on a PhD in philosophy. He still planned to teach in Japan, but instead went to Germany and then a college in Indiana. He then moved east to study at Harvard for a second PhD, but during his orals he had a nervous breakdown. He left Harvard without his coveted degree and the academic success he hoped would follow. His every turn seemed to be thwarted.

In 1938, though, Kelly underwent a profound spiritual change. He felt a new sense of purpose and spirit in his life. His lectures and writing reflected this inner growth. His essays produced a great interest among people interested in the mystical spiritual life. His work from this period—arrived at because of closed doors—resulted in a book that continues to point women and men to God and invites them into the depths of God's love.

While few of us will have as many closed doors as Kelly did, we can learn from his experience. Look back on your life and ask yourself, where has something closed that led to another opening? Where was God in that closing—and in the new opening?

LOSTNESS HELPS US PONDER

When we are committed to following the sacred compass, God commits himself to us. As we ask God to honor that commitment, we can also ask ourselves questions that invite reflection:

- ◆ What are you feeling?
- ◆ What are these feelings telling you?
- ◆ Why do you call what you're feeling "lost"?

By digging into questions like those, you can get to the heart of your feelings and can move on to other penetrating questions:

- ◆ What do you need in order to gain clarity?
- ◆ How can you move from this place?
- ◆ Should you move from this place?
- ◆ Who can help you hear God's word for you?

LOSTNESS CAN ENGAGE OUR CREATIVITY

Lostness is also a good time to engage our creativity. Research shows an interesting link between dark or lost times and creativity. Though being creative in such a time may seem beyond our ability, it is during the lostness that we most need to tap into our creative selves. The rewards will surprise us.

Think about what kind of sound track would accompany what you're feeling at this time—Wagner's "Ride of the Valkyries," or Over the Rhine's "Nothing is Innocent."

Consider your religious training:

◆ Can you imagine certain biblical characters or saints experiencing what you feel?

◆ How would, or did, they deal with those feelings?

A friend of mine told me about a lost time in her life when she felt like Jonah. She felt as if she'd been swallowed by a giant fish that took her some place she didn't want to go to do something she really didn't want to do, even it was what God wanted. Engaging her creative energies in that association helped her sense God's presence.

Listen to your conversations and thoughts. It is especially important in times of deep feeling to let your life speak to you. Listen for words that you use frequently and images, questions, desires, or challenges that come up repeatedly:

◆ What do they tell you about where you are?

◆ Do they say you are where you think you are— or somewhere different?

Lostness is a good time to pray in color, do guided meditations, and write—to participate in things that give you life, both emotionally and spiritually. Be expressive. Don't hold back. Give your spirit free reign and trust that God will receive what needs receiving and discard the rest. Lostness is a time to use creativity to teach us how to release control and let our creator God work through and in us.

LOSTNESS AND HOPE

"I have found life is easier," a friend of mine said, "when you give up all hope." At one level, his saying that didn't surprise me. His life had seemed dark for a few years. First, his son died. Then, his beloved wife died a couple of years later in the same intensive care unit. Still, his statement took me aback. I always think of this guy as a person of extreme creativity, vitality, and imagination. He's the sort who seems to bring ideas to life in new and exciting ways. That, to me, embodies the essence of hope.

As I later reflected on what he said, I thought there were two ways to look at his statement. One way is as an expression of despair—an "abandon all hope ye who enter here" sort of thinking. After all, as one wag put it, none of us get out of here alive.

The other way is to see this statement as a positive truth. Maybe we need to give up hope because the hope we have is placed in the wrong hands. I like to cling tight to control—I doubt that I'm alone in that—because I want things to work out the way I want them to work out. That's natural. But hope like that is based on three flawed premises.

Hope and Human Intellect

The first flawed premise is the wisdom of our intellect. We want rational answers, and when we can't come up with them, we tend to give up hope. We want to understand so badly (and that is exactly is how I often understand . . . "so badly"), to put life and its complexities (especially in hard times) into some kind of rational formula that we can comprehend. While we are marvels of God's engineering, with amazing abilities of accumulating knowledge, there is no way we can comprehend every aspect of everything in the cosmos. If that understanding is the basis for our hope in the sacred compass, then we're bound to feel lost.

Hope and Human Emotion

The second flawed premise is emotion. Emotion has us screaming, "Why is this happening?" Twenty-five years ago, I stood in the doorway of my family's spare bedroom, staring at the wasted body of my best friend who had blown his brains out with a revolver. The question wasn't intellectual then; it was pure emotion. Even though I hardly said a word, deep streams of anguish welled up from my heart, forcing their way through every part of me. "Why, why, why?" And I felt his silence mock me. I would never again ride with him on the back of his motorcycle, or laugh at his practical jokes, or share the life we had shared since fifth grade. Grief, rage, hurt all raced through me, threatening to snuff out hope. Emotions, as wonderful as they are when the sun is shining and the future is bright, are not a good barometer for hope. For, soon, a low front will sweep across our lives, driving us into the doubt of storms.

Hope and Human Perspective

The third flawed premise is the limitation of our human perspective. We tend to perceive our world as consisting only of that which we can see, taste, hear, smell, and touch. We say that we are spiritual beings, and at times we live into the reality of that statement. But many times we live as if that truth weren't true. Even though Jesus, Paul, and writers throughout the ages tell us that we are not just of a physical realm but a spiritual one as well, and we nod our head and soul in agreement, we often live as if we don't believe it. We cling tightly to this life and its ways because this life is what we know. In C.S. Lewis's space trilogy, one of the agents of God (though neither God nor the agent are referred to in those terms in the story) is talking to a human and says:

You thick one, have told me nothing of yourself, so I will tell it to you. In your own world you have attained great wisdom . . . but in all other things you have the mind of an animal. The darkness in your own mind filled you with fear. It is the Bent One [as he calls evil] who wastes your lives and befouls them with flying from what you know will overtake you in the end. If you were subjects of [God] you would have peace.

Perhaps our limitations, which keep us focused on the visible, keep us from peace and from hope, which truly lies in a realm beyond our own.

Saint Paul says, "Whatever we may have to go through now is less than nothing compared with the magnificent future God has planned for us. The whole creation is on tiptoe to see the wonderful sight of the sons of God coming into their own." And therein lies the positive truth in my friend's statement about giving up hope.

LOSTNESS CAN LEAD US TO TRUE HOPE

When we give up a hope placed in the wrong things, we have cleared the way for the true hope. This true hope is not based in intellect, emotion, or our perception of reality, though in fact true hope includes portions of all three. This hope, according to St. Paul, is that "in the end the whole of created life will be rescued from the tyranny of change and decay, and have its share in that magnificent liberty which can only belong to the children of God."

Paul goes on to say that "it is plain to anyone with eyes to see that at the present time all created life groans in a sort of universal travail . . . painful tension. . . . [But] we know that to those who love God, who are called according to his plan, everything that happens fits into a pattern for good." Paul is not saying that everything that happens is good. He is saying that God fits everything that happens into a pattern that turns out for good—a tapestry that is perhaps woven of broken threads.

When we give up hope, as we tend to understand it in this world, we find life easier because we no longer have to make it turn out right. We couldn't if we tried, and we acknowledge that we do not have the power to do so. We then rest in God, who is for us when all else is against us.

We find true hope in trusting the promise that God is for us. Psalm 139 gives us the foundation for believing in this round of God's love even in the darkest of times.

O LORD, you have searched me and known me. You know when I sit down and when I rise up; you discern my thoughts from far away. You search out my path and my lying down, and are acquainted with all my ways. Even before a word is on my tongue, O LORD, you know it completely. You hem me in, behind and before, and lay your hand upon me. Such knowledge is too wonderful for me; it is so high that I cannot attain it.

God is with us. God knows us. We can never completely understand these truths, on good days and on bad days. As the psalmist says—"Such knowledge is too wonderful for me; it is so high that I cannot attain it."

That is not to say we need to be blindly faithful or that we can't scream out our questions or wonder why or feel lost. Such honest expressions are part of who we are. But following the sacred compass, even when we feel lost, means placing a bold confidence in that which we cannot see with our physical eyes. Following God means saying no to the fearfulness crowding our hearts. Spiritual trusting means clinging to the love of God—and hope.

The Gestapo imprisoned French dramatist and novelist Tristan Bernard and his wife during World War II. "The time of fear is over," Bernard told his wife at their arrest. "Now comes the time of hope."

LOSTNESS IS DIVINE MYSTERY

The sacred compass moves us toward God. We move not toward that which can be fully known, but that which is in large part unknown. God and God's ultimate path for us are mystery at its deepest level. This mystery is the reason we cannot find adequate answers to the question of why, if God is loving and kind and all knowing and all powerful, there is pain and suffering in this world. Why does sickness and death steal the ones we love? Why do terrorists slaughter innocent office workers on bright September mornings?

God is mysterious. Hence, comes faith. Faith is not a call to understanding. It is a call to trust. Faith asks us, as the southern writer Flannery O'Connor once said, to have "the kind of mind that is willing to have its sense of mystery deepened by contact with reality, and its sense of reality deepened by contact with mystery"—that mystery, of course, being God.

Many of us are uneasy with allowing God to have that much mystery. Such mystery leads into places where, sacred compass in hand or not, we feel lost. We prefer a tamer God-guide, one that fits our ideal emotionally and intellectually. But God is completely other. Following and trusting that one who is completely other takes us to places in our lostness where we can say, "I don't know why, but I do know this . . . 'Where can I go from your spirit? Or where can I flee from your presence?'"

We follow the sacred compass in no small part so that we can be searched by and known by the one who enfolds us whether we are in the light or in the dark of lostness. We follow so that we can learn to trust. In the words of poet Thomas R. Smith:

It's like so many other things in life
to which you must say no or yes.
So you take your car to the new mechanic.
Sometimes the best thing to do is trust.

The package left with the disreputable-looking
clerk, the check gulped by the night deposit,
the envelope passed by dozens of strangers—
all show up at their intended destinations.
The theft that could have happened doesn't.
Wind finally gets where it was going
through the snowy trees, and the river, even
when frozen, arrives at the right place.

And sometimes you sense how faithfully your life is delivered,
even though you can't read the address.

God faithfully delivers our lives, even when we can't read the
address. Trusting that takes us to a place where we realize that
lostness is part of following our sacred compass. Lostness also
reminds us that we may only see part of the path at a time. We
may soon break out of the underbrush into an alpine meadow
replete with a flowing waterfall and cheerful fellow pilgrims
waiting for us. Or we may run into a grizzly bear.

Regardless, God is with us always. No matter how joyous
life is. No matter how painful it feels. The steadfast, faithful,
loving presence of all presences attends our pilgrim path.

SIX

WEST OF EDEN

What If the Way Takes Us to Unexpected Places?

I RAQI CHILDREN FOUND TOM FOX'S BODY riddled with bullets and wrapped in a blanket and black plastic bags. Fox was in Iraq on a mission to help end violence. Following the sacred compass led him to a place he may have prepared for, but still did not expect.

A former musician in the United States Marine Corps Band, Fox left Virginia for Iraq in 2004 as part of a Christian Peacemaking Team mission. He believed that Christians needed to devote the same discipline and self-sacrifice to nonviolent peacemaking that armies devote to war. Fox's work included visiting imprisoned Iraqis and accompanying medical shipments to clinics and hospitals. While he may not have known what to expect from following his leading, he was fully aware of the dangers. Blogging from Iraq, Fox wrote, "Does that mean I walk into a raging battle to confront the soldiers? Does that mean I walk the streets of Baghdad with a sign saying 'American for the Taking'? No to both counts. But if Jesus and Gandhi are right, then I am asked to risk my life and if I lose it to be as forgiving as they were when murdered by the forces of Satan."

In November 2005, the Swords of Righteousness Brigade took Fox and three other members of his Christian Peacemaking Team hostage. In March 2006, his bullet-filled body was discovered.

Tom Fox found what countless Christians have discovered—that following the sacred compass can take us to unexpected and difficult places.

WE FOLLOW THE GOD OF THE UNEXPECTED

God Is Not Always What We Expect

The longer we walk with God, the more we find that we are not called to follow a gentle Jesus, meek and mild—but rather a power that often churns us inside and out. As Martin Bell, an Episcopal priest, writes about Jesus' disciples in *The Way of the Wolf*, "To have experienced the Christ . . . must have been like stepping into the path of a hurricane."

Can you think of a time when God was like that for you—if not a hurricane, then some other unexpected, mighty force?

God Unexpectedly Leads Us into Bad Weather

God sometimes leads us into the path of a holy hurricane. We may find ourselves in difficult, dangerous, or frightening places because, in our seeking God's will, we sense that something is needed from us or is awry with the world and are moved to respond. There are times that the voice of Christ calls us out of our comfort in the same way Jesus called Peter out of the boat and onto the water. Certainly, that was true for Tom Fox. Our hearts hear the call, we check our compass and move to follow it, and our path takes us into a storm.

We Are Unexpectedly Transformed

God's call may involve transformation of an entire life—such as Fox's doffing his fatigues and donning the garments of peace. When we hear God's call, we pray with William Bright:

> O God, by whom the meek are guided in judgment and light riseth up in darkness, grant us, amid our doubts and uncertainties, the grace to ask what thou wouldst have us do, that the spirit of wisdom may save us from false choices, that in thy light we may see light and in thy straight path we may not stumble. Amen.

The unexpected places also mold and shape us into our more authentic selves—the selves God created us to be. We not only go through hard times but we grow through hard times. Now, before you turn that into some sort of bumper sticker platitude, think about it. Where have you discovered the growing edges of your life—while lying on the beach in the sun or scaling a difficult mountain in your life? Where and when did you grow?

Part of the purpose of way opening, even when it opens in unexpected, difficult places, is to help us discover our true selves—the selves that bring us inner contentment and life with God.

God Unexpectedly Shows Up in Others

Another gift of finding ourselves in unexpected places can be God's loving care for us coming from the kindnesses of friends and family. As Edward Milligan wrote:

> Isolation of spirit . . comes to most—perhaps all of us—at one time or another. There are times in our lives when the tides of faith seem far out, times of dryness, times when we do not feel the comfort and guidance of God's hand. . . . [W]ithin, we feel the agonies of isolation and the longing for light to lighten our darkness. I can think with thankfulness of Friends who have brought light to my darkness—perhaps a single sentence, a friendly letter, a walk on the downs: their help was perhaps given unconsciously, but it was because they were sensitive to God's leadings that they were able to do it. Do we seek to be the channels of God's love and caring? "Caring matters most."

Let others be the love of God for you, the way you may be called upon to be for them someday.

UNEXPECTED PLACES TEACH US TO TRUST

As we grow in our ability to follow the sacred compass, we often travel into deeper and more difficult places. If, that is, we are serious about following Christ.

At first, the sacred compass usually takes us some place easy, places resembling green pastures and still waters, like the leading I felt to sign a letter advocating dignity and just compensation as essential human rights for janitors and other low-wage workers in our town. That was pretty safe. Nothing life-threatening there.

Then, as part of limbering up our spiritual muscles, God may unexpectedly take us to a harder place. This may surprise us—though it shouldn't. God has given us plenty of warning that it could happen. The Bible is full of stories of people whose sacred compass led them to unexpected places:

- Jonah and the belly of a great fish
- Daniel and a lions' den
- Mary and a manger and, later, at the foot of the cross
- Saul/Paul being led blind into Damascus

One thing to remember about following the sacred compass is that God is always with us. That's what Jonah, Daniel, and Saul/Paul found. Jonah discovered God with him when he was trying his best to go the opposite direction than his sacred compass was leading. Saul/Paul learned that God was with him when God showed him that what he thought was God's will was actually the opposite. Daniel's faithfulness found God with him in the danger of the lions' den. Mary's trust in God's presence led her to pray:

> My soul magnifies the Lord,
>   and my spirit rejoices in God my Savior,
>   for he has regarded the low estate of his handmaiden.
> For behold, henceforth all generations will call me blessed;
>   for he who is mighty has done great things for me,
>   and holy is his name.
> And his mercy is on those who fear him from generation to generation.
> He has shown strength with his arm,
> he has scattered the proud in the imagination of their hearts,
> he has put down the mighty from their thrones,
>   and exalted those of low degree;
> he has filled the hungry with good things,
>   and the rich he has sent empty away.
> He has helped his servant Israel,

> in remembrance of his mercy,
> as he spoke to our fathers,
> to Abraham and to his posterity for ever.

Seeing God at work this way does not negate the tragedies and sorrows of life. Rather, it reminds us that we have limited sight and reasoning in this world. Leading us to an unexpected place is one way God helps us to strengthen our interior lives. We learn to:

- pray
- praise
- repent
- listen with our soul's ears
- look for God at work

and do a host of other things that transform our spirit. That transformation leads us to an unexpected place of living with joy in the midst of heartache. Walking with God in the unexpected places teaches us an assurance that we are always and in all ways loved and cared for, not just when life is light and easy.

God may take us places where we're scared out of our spiritual wits, but we are safe with God. As we find ourselves moving into unforeseen difficult times or situations, we need to remind ourselves that God is right—and trustworthy. Even when we can't sense or see the "rightness," we can learn to rest in God's trustworthiness, though it may take our whole lives to learn to do so.

Many pilgrims have found that Jesus' yoke is easy and the burden is light only in retrospect. What makes for an easy yoke and light burden is learning to place confidence in God's leadings, even when they are unexpected. Such confidence does not deny the reality of the pain and sadness that may come our way. But we recognize that an unexpected difficult trail can stretch our soul in ways that a gentle hike across green pastures and beside still waters never can. An uphill, hazard-strewn path takes us to a place where we see that our strength is not sufficient. We learn to surrender our control and step into God's loving embrace.

As we yield to God, we discover how to live in God's love and joy and peace. The farther we follow our sacred compass, the more we find ourselves rejoicing that God is with us, even in places we think we'd rather not go. It's okay to say, "I'm willing to go, God. Just match my pace. Don't leave me in the spiritual dust." God stays with us. When we say, "Wait for me." God says, "Okay," even while nudging us along. And when we look back down the pilgrim path and see God at work and with us, we can say with Teresa of Avila:

Although I have often abandoned you, O Lord, you have never abandoned me. Your hand of love is always outstretched towards me, even when I stubbornly look the other way. And your gentle voice constantly calls me, even when I obstinately refuse to listen.

WE ASK UNEXPECTED QUESTIONS

How did I get here? I wondered, wading through waist-high weeds and the moist summer Indiana air that swarmed with mosquitoes. I knew what I was doing there: I was meeting with our builder and talking about the house we were building. But how I got there was completely beside me.

I looked through the tall grasses and weeds and spotted my bobble-headed wife. Her head bounced up through the weeds, down into the tall grass. She stepped back onto the sort-of farm lane above the creek, a huge smile stretched across her face. "Isn't this gorgeous?" she asked. "Aren't you just so excited? This is paradise." *Excited* and *paradise* were words that had not occurred to me. *Hot. Sweaty. Itchy. Debt-laden.* Those words occurred to me, but not *excited* and *paradise*.

Nancy's a farm girl, and this land was part of her family's farm. I grew up a city boy. I like the city. I work in the city. Now, here I was, miles away from my downtown office and over fifteen hundred feet away from the closest road with no blacktop in sight. *How did I get here?*

I wonder if Adam wondered the same thing upon finding himself waking in Eden. "And the LORD God formed man of the dust of the ground, and breathed into his nostrils the breath of life; and man became a living soul. And the LORD God planted a garden eastward in Eden; and there he put the man whom he had formed." Yes, the Bible says, "And out of the ground made the LORD God to grow every tree that is pleasant to the sight, and good for food," which must have made for a lovely sight, but I still keep wondering if Adam asked himself, *How did I get here?*

In spite of my anguish that day with the builder, an overgrown farm field is the sort of place that following the sacred compass takes most of us—not places of martyrdom or violent harm. While these kinds of unexpected places may not threaten our physical life, they each turn our life upside down. That's how I felt that day in the field: as I was about to be turned upside down. That feeling was behind my question, *How did I get here?*

What I've since discovered is that this is not entirely the right question because it implies that the journey is all about me. It's not. It's *about* me, but not all about me. It's also about:

- Nancy
- our families
- wildlife crawling across the land
- the home we open up to others in hospitality
- and all the other connections I have

Inside, I knew this truth, but I struggled to come to grips with it. I was not the center of even my universe. As Nancy reminds me, it's only one sixth–billionth about me. Which is

what made the "How did *I* get here" question the wrong one.
The right questions were:

- *How did* we *get here?*
- Why *did we get here?*
- What *are we here for?*
- *What are we going to do about it?*

Those questions began to open my focus. They reminded
me of the communal nature of discernment and calling. If
the sacred compass led me to the job that brought us back to
central Indiana, then the sacred compass brought us this way
so Nancy could to be close to her father and some of her literal
roots. It also brought us back so I could follow my leading to
form a worship-sharing group. It also brought us back so I
would be forced to slow my life by spending hours in a tractor
seat or walking our dog in the woods. These are the kinds of
unexpected places that the sacred compass leads us, inviting us
to live in harmony with a sentiment by Gordon Matthews:

We must learn to put our trust in God and the leadings
of the Spirit. I am only slowly learning to dwell in the
place where leadings come from. That is a place of love
and joy and peace, even in the midst of pain. The more I
dwell in that place, the easier it is to smile, because I am
no longer afraid.

If we dwell in the presence of God, we shall be led by the spirit. We do well to remember that being led by the spirit depends not so much upon God, who is always there to lead us, as upon our willingness to be led. We need to be willing to be led into the dark as well as through green pastures and by still waters. We do not need to be afraid of the dark, because God is there. Let us walk with a smile into the dark.

Now, walking with a smile into the dark—the unexpected places—is not something that comes easily to me. I still look over my shoulder to see who's following me up the stairs when I shut off the basement light. Yet, the thought of following the sacred compass into the dark with a smile reminds us that life is not all about us. Life is about us and God and. . . . We each have to fill in that blank as we discern our calling.

DOORS UNEXPECTEDLY OPEN—THEN CLOSE

Another aspect of the way taking us unexpected places is that way may seem to open, only to then close. This was the case for me about a year after I joined the Indianapolis Center for Congregations. The founding director took me to coffee one morning and told me he'd accepted a new position and would be leaving. Friends soon began asking me if I was going to apply to be the new president. Nancy and I talked about the position. Our leading was that I shouldn't apply.

But then someone nominated me for the position. Nancy and I prayed for God's will to be done. We prayed for the board to choose the right person. We also prayed that if I was not the right person, the way would close. Way kept opening. In spite of those prayers, I began to get excited about the possibility of leading the center.

By the time the call came announcing another candidate's selection, I felt as though something I wanted had been taken away from me. At the same time, I had a certain amount of clarity. I had been praying that the board would choose the right person. I knew the board members as people of deep faith and commitment. So I had to trust their discernment—it was a discernment I'd been praying for.

The *why* part was harder. Why had God allowed the process to go as far as it did, if I was not to be the one? Why was I nominated after I had decided not to apply? Why did my interviews go so well? I felt a little bit like the guy in a *New Yorker* cartoon by J.B. Handelsman. He's kneeling by his bed in his pajamas, looking heavenward, and saying, "I asked You, in the nicest possible way, to make me a better person, but apparently You couldn't be bothered."

All these thoughts and more raced through my brain, and the word I kept hearing inside was, *trust.* So, slowly I tried to do just that. A week after I let my friends know I didn't get the job, one of them called. "I was praying you wouldn't get the job," she said. "You were happy where you were, your health was better, you were writing more. I think you're where you're supposed to be. Mad at me?" she asked. "Nope," I said. "Just bewildered at this point." "You'll be fine," she said. And she was right.

As I look back on the process, it seems that it was a test of faith. For much of my life I've been a "striver"—the classic type-A person looking to get ahead. After some severe personal crises, though, I began a major reassessment of my life. I decided I wanted to live more in God and less in myself. Part of living more in God was recognizing that the needs of my ego easily got in the way of any good I might want to do. So, I intentionally tried to take positions where I helped others flourish. I worked at quenching my need to be front and center.

The presidential search process was, I think, God asking me, "Are you serious about this humility thing? Do you really want to do what I want you to do rather than what your ego wants you to do?"

I thought about that recently while watching the movie *Evan Almighty*. While the story of Evan Baxter, a newscaster-turned-congressman whom God calls to build an ark, is hardly a cinematic classic, one part really spoke to me. Early in the film, Evan tries to pray. He's a novice at praying and the best he can come up with is a prayer to spend more time with his family.

Then comes an encounter with God, and his whole life changes. Biblical robes and a John-the-Baptist hairdo replace his tailored suits and carefully coiffed hair. Loads of lumber are dumped in his driveway. One day he asks God what any of this has to do with answering his prayer for time with his family. God answers with questions:

> Let me ask you something. If someone prays for patience, you think God gives them patience? Or does he give them the opportunity to be patient? If he prayed for courage, does God give him courage, or does he give him opportunities to be courageous? If someone prayed for the family to be closer, do you think God zaps them with warm fuzzy feelings, or does he give them opportunities to love each other?

Does God give me humility, or does God give me opportunities to be humble? It's a question I need to hear. It's a question you may need to hear, too. Look back on your life—especially to those times when doors seemed to slam shut—and ask:

- ◆ Did you pray for something, and then God gave you the opportunity to learn it?
- ◆ What lessons have you learned from doors closing?
- ◆ How has a closed door been an answer— even if unexpected—to a prayer?

THE UNEXPECTED SAYS STOP

One thing we can do when we find ourselves so far west of Eden that we can't see any hint of paradise, is to stop and check our sacred compass. Are we on the proper path? The answer may be yes. Just because a way is hard doesn't mean that it's the wrong path. But coming to an unexpected place is still a good time to check the compass by asking:

- ◆ Where do you see life in this place?
- ◆ Do you sense God here?
- ◆ Where is love?
- ◆ Do you see light?

If you don't see life, light, love, and God in this unexpected place, you might want to look for another path—one that leads you to those things. Where God is, there is life. Where love is, there is light. Where you see life, light, love, and God in an unexpected place, you're probably on the right path—even if it's a hard one.

There are more questions you can ask yourself—questions that are true to your heart and spiritual path. That's what Tom Fox did, and he found his calling in the hard places, even while questioning them:

How do I stay with the pain and suffering and not be overwhelmed? How do I resist the welling up of rage towards the perpetrators of violence? How do I keep from disconnecting from or becoming numb to the pain?

After eight months, I am no clearer than I was when I began. In fact I have to struggle harder and harder each day against my desire to move away or become numb. Simply staying with the pain of others doesn't seem to create any healing or transformation. Yet there seems to be no other first step into the realm of compassion than to not step away.

"Becoming intimate with the queasy feeling of being in the middle of nowhere makes our hearts more tender. When we are brave enough to stay in the nowhere place then compassion arises spontaneously." [Fox is quoting Buddhist teacher Pema Chodron's book *The Places That Scare You.*]

Being in the middle of nowhere really does create a very queasy feeling and yet so many spiritual teachers say it is the only authentic place to be. Not staking out any ground for myself creates the possibility of standing with anyone. The middle of nowhere is the one place where compassion can be discovered. The constant challenge is recognizing that my true country of origin is the middle of nowhere.

As Fox found, the hard way was more than a time of questioning—it was also a time of growing.

UNEXPECTED PLACES MAKE GOOD REFLECTING POOLS

The path leading us to unexpected places offers an opportunity for reflection—a time to reexamine where we are and discern if we are on the correct path. It is a time to:

◆ examine our souls
◆ test our motives

- ◆ look at the blessings and gifts we received by coming this way
- ◆ ask what we would have missed if we'd taken another route

Reflection often reminds us that all good things come from God, and that God works for us even when we don't recognize it or find ourselves in unexpected places. We often don't think this way. Because of our human pain and anguish, we may, at first, be unable or unwilling to see any good coming from unexpected places. But, as Edward Grubb wrote, "Trouble of soul can teach us things that raptures never could—not only patience and perseverance, but humility and sympathy with others." And, I would add, trouble of soul teaches us about the never ceasing presence of God.

WE UNEXPECTEDLY BECOME WITNESSES

Tom Fox continues to be a witness. His blog, "Waiting In the Light," opens with a quotation from George Fox, "Be patterns, be examples in every country, place, or nation that you visit, so that your bearing and life might communicate with all people. Then you'll happily walk across the earth to evoke that of God in everybody. So that you will be seen as a blessing in their eyes and you will receive a blessing from that of God within them." Tom's writings speak to the ongoing reality of war that our planet faces and to our call to be healers. His life bears witness to the act of following our sacred compass, even when it leads to unexpected places.

◆

Was following the sacred compass worth it for Tom Fox? If we asked him, perhaps he would assure us that trusting in the one who led him made it worth it. He trusted his guide. He trusted the story God told him. He believed that, behind all of our stories, life has meaning,

that things that happen to people happen not just by accident like leaves being blown off a tree by the wind but that there is order and purpose deep down behind them or inside them and they are leading us not just anywhere but somewhere.

SEVEN

TRAVELER'S AID
Offering Assistance to Others Along the Way

I REALLY NEED TO SEE YOU." Jane was calling, and she sounded urgent. "Could you meet me for lunch tomorrow?" Her words worried me. Jane and I have been friends for over twenty years. I scanned my calendar and we agreed to meet the next day. From the time I hung up the phone to our lunch appointment the next day, I wondered what was wrong. I feared the worse—were she and her husband, Jeff, having problems? Did she have some major health issue?

I got to the restaurant first. Jane came in a few minutes later. She looked untroubled—a good sign. We made small talk. "How's Nancy?" "How are the kids?" Finally, testing, I asked, "How's Jeff?" "He's fine. He's really busy with the police force and law school." The waiter came. We ordered.

"So . . . ?" I said.

"Well, I need your advice. I've been offered the opportunity to get back into newspaper journalism." I breathed a relieved sigh and sat back to listen. This was good big stuff, not bad big stuff.

WE'RE DEEPER THAN WE THINK

Calls like Jane's are part of our pilgrim's path. As we follow the sacred compass, we often grow into a reputation of being someone to turn to for spiritual counsel. Quakers call such people "weighty" friends." Weight, used this way, doesn't mean pounds, but rather a depth of sacred wisdom. Weighty friends are spiritually wise.

The idea that we are spiritually weighty is not, as the Quakers wryly say, "a thought that would occur to me." We rarely see ourselves as wise, but we all know other people who live so close to God that going to them would be the closest thing on this earth to going to God. We just rarely see ourselves as being one of those people.

J.I. Packer, in *Knowing God*, tells the story of an academic friend of his who lost a chance for advancement after wrangling with some church VIPs. Packer reports him as saying, "But it doesn't matter . . . for I've known God and they haven't."

"I've known God and they haven't," sounds pretty arrogant. Who does this fellow think he is? Instead of being arrogant, though, he may be making a simple statement of fact. His words might be those of a person who lives so close to God that they are as normal as my saying, "I know Nancy." That's the sort of intimacy with God that following the sacred compass gives us. It's an intimacy that others may recognize, and so they come to us to hear a good word from God.

SHARE YOUR GIFT

Most of us do not see ourselves as spiritually wise (even those of us who think we know everything!), and so we are loath to give advice. But, as St. Paul urged Timothy, "Do not neglect the gift that is in you." Part of our gift is sharing the wisdom we've acquired. Sharing this wisdom, though, is not about giving advice. Instead, it's about listening to others and helping them discover their way. A call like Jane's didn't come because she wanted me to give her The Answer. She called because she knew that, no matter how many times I've failed, I try to walk close to God. She was confident that I would listen to her and to God.

Listening to and with a friend is a gift we share. Listening says to someone we care about, "Here we are, you and I, and I hope a third, Christ, is in our midst." Being invited to share our gift is also a call:

- to create a safe place for spiritual investigation
- to embrace hope
- to hear the Spirit
- to encourage faithful obedience

Sharing our gift honors the truth that God gives each of us opportunities to share spiritually with others on the pilgrim path. Sharing in this way is part of following our sacred compass.

POINT TO CHRIST

Congregational leaders may find themselves called to fill this role more often than others. Pastors, especially, are asked, "What should I do?" Two local pastors and I had lunch recently, when the topic of being asked for spiritual guidance came up. We talked about this as we munched on big pretzels, rye rolls, and other good German food. One pastor said that such questions, even after sixteen years in the ministry, disconcerted him. He knows that as a pastor (and authority figure) he encounters people in his congregation who come to him for a "thus saith the Lord" sort of statement. That was something he didn't feel comfortable offering. He asked what I did. I told him that I've finally learned to drop the "thus saith the Lord" statements and instead offer the more open "thus asketh the Brent."

I do that because I struggle to hear what God has to say to me, and I'm not going to presume to know what God has to say to others. So, I mostly ask questions. I direct my friends to Christ their Inner Teacher. I point them to God's wisdom. I ask them what the Holy Spirit is doing in their life. Any of us—pastor or not—can offer these gifts when invited into a friend's spiritual discernment.

As we talked, I thought about a story that Will D. Campbell, the offbeat Baptist radical told me. I phoned to invite him to Earlham School of Religion's writing colloquium. As we talked, he mentioned that he'd been at Earlham before. D. Elton

Trueblood, one of the college's leading minds and author of more than thirty books, had invited Campbell to speak. "We shall gather in silence," intoned Trueblood, "and then when the Spirit moves you, you shall stand and give your address." Campbell, a sprite-ly fellow in body and spirit and wit, impishly asked, "How will I know that the Spirit moves me?" "When you shall feel my elbow in your side," replied Trueblood.

While most of us would never equate our nudging somebody with an elbow to the prompting of the Holy Spirit, it is easy to get the two mixed up when we're in a position of providing advice or counsel. Appearing wise is ego-gratifying, especially if the person is prone to take our advice. We need to remember that we're not there to give advice or solve a problem. That may be what people who come to us want, and not meeting that desire is difficult, but we are there to listen, to ask questions, and to point them to the answers God has for them—not that we have for them. As singer-songwriter Carrie Newcomer, who also facilitates clearness groups, noted:

> The biggest problems occur when a listener cannot keep themselves from giving advice. Often it is well meaning with a desire to nurture and problem solve. But what happens is the person seeking discernment will shut down and the process stops. I've found the more I reinforce that this process is about respecting the question and trusting and believing in the abilities of the person seeking

discernment to eventually get where they need to be, the better the process proceeds.

SPACE FOR GOD

Being asked to share in friends' spiritual journeys lets us help them open space for God's light to break through. We share our spiritual wisdom to help our friends experience God. On the PBS series *Searching for God in America,* Rabbi Harold Kushner tells the following story that illuminates just that point:

> A couple of summers ago, a woman asked me, "How do I get my eleven-year-old son to believe in God?" I said, "It's the wrong question. . . . This is the question you should be asking, 'How do I get my eleven-year-old son to experience God? How do I get my eleven-year-old son to recognize that he has just met God?' "

Helping friends meet God is at the heart of being a spiritual friend. We get to help them see that God is there to give them the wisdom and direction. We point the way to God.

Prayerful listening helps us create space for God. Keep your soul in an attitude of prayer while your heart and mind focus on those you are counseling. Your attention needs to be on them, not yourself. Stay in a place of prayerful listening and refrain from offering answers. Speak only when words will move the person along or clarify something he or she has said. Use what words you need to encourage your friends to focus on the way forward. Instead of making statements or giving opinions, offer mostly questions—ones that are simple and nondirective. Ask questions slowly and avoid asking whatever pops into your head. Give the right questions time to come to you with some sense of insistence. Use only those that have simmered in your soul, such as:

- What do they need answered in order to move forward?
- Do they feel free *not* to make a decision if they do not reach a clear discernment?
- Are they seeking confirmation?
- How will they know they have the answer they seek?

While those you counsel might ask what you would do, sharing too much of your own experiences and insights can distract them from the things they need to attend. You want them to listen to God through you—not just to you.

Amazing things happen when we refrain from giving advice and enter into listening to our friend and God. For one, we hear God's truth for ourselves as well as our friend. We find ourselves reconnecting with joy. We see the pilgrim path opening in fresh, energizing ways for us. We discover that participating in such holy work transforms us, and we pray with Christina Rossetti:

Lord Jesus, merciful and patient,
Grant us grace, I beseech thee, ever

To teach in a teachable spirit;
Learning along with those we teach,
And learning from them whenever thou so pleasest.

LED TO OFFER A WORD

Sometimes we are invited to share spiritual help. At other times, we are led to offer a word without being asked. This is an important leading that requires special care. We need to spend time in discernment to ensure that we offer words from a sense of calling and not from some ego need. Such a leading shows, though, that as we've followed our sacred compass we've had experiences that informed and shaped us. These experiences gave us wisdom. Times come when we find ourselves led to share that wisdom.

I experienced such a time recently. Some tormentors have beset a friend of mine. My friend told me he felt the time had come to confront the people who were demeaning him to other people. I was uneasy about this confrontation because I didn't think it would solve his problem.

One night I had some insight into a way he might deal with this issue. I tested the idea on Nancy. She agreed, so I sent my friend an e-mail telling him my thought. He didn't ask me to do that, and offering that kind of advice took me outside my comfort zone. Offering advice runs counter to what I said in the previous section about keeping yourself to questions only.

The difference here was that in this situation I was not asked for advice. Instead, God led me to share. So I did. My friend thanked me. I don't know whether he followed my advice, and I don't particularly care if he did or not. That wasn't the point for me. The point was that I was faithful and shared the leading I'd been given. The rest was up to my friend and God.

OFFERING A WARNING

In addition to words of direction, we might be called to offer words of warning. We might see friends heading down what appears to be a wrong road—making a decision that could be disastrous or doing things that could put them emotionally and physically at risk. Sometimes we need to keep silent. Other times we may be led to speak. The primary test again is motive: Why do we feel a need to speak? Because we know what's best? Or because God's love compels us? It is important that warning words come from God's heart more than our ego, lest they sound harsh or judgmental. Ego-inspired words won't be received in the spirit of God's loving. George Fox gives good advice when he says:

And all such as behold their brother or sister in a transgression, go not in rough, light, or upbraiding spirit to reprove or admonish him or her, but in the power of the Lord, and the spirit of the Lamb, and in the wisdom and love of the Truth.

Still, this type of loving confrontation is not something we feel comfortable doing. And it shouldn't be. If it's easy, we've probably not listened to God. Sounding a warning is something to be approached prayerfully and reluctantly, but obediently. Do not worry about whether or not your words are heeded. You are the messenger—not the "fixer." God and your friend will do the work that needs to happen.

WALKING ALONGSIDE

Following our sacred compass may also lead us to walk alongside others during their dark time. Our souls might be bathed in sunshine when a leading comes to stand with friends enduring a difficult night. We must pay attention to the leadings that urge us to reach out, subtle as they may be. Otherwise, we may find ourselves lamenting like George Gorman:

I recall with sadness my insensitivity years ago to the difficulties of one of my closest friends. His marriage was breaking up and although I saw him regularly during the period, I was completely unaware of his unhappiness. With such a lesson in my background, I should have learnt by now—yet I still manage to tread hard on tender toes. All this makes me even more certain that if we are to speak to others, we first need to learn to listen to them with sensitivity.

This learning to listen to our friends—and God—with sensitivity takes us to a place where we truly share in our friends' lives.

CLEARNESS COMMITTEES

Besides personal discernment, Quakers have another method of helping people follow their sacred compass. We form a group and call it a clearness committee. Clearness committees have assisted seeking Friends in finding clearness in everything from confirming marriage partners to making career choices. These committees can be used to make any decision that calls for spiritual discernment.

Listening to Christ

The concept behind a clearness committee is simple: it is a gathering of a group of spiritual friends with the holy aspiration to help a person reach a sense of sacred clearness. The committee's work has some similarity to one-on-one spiritual friendship, in that it is nondirective and attentive. Clearness committees operate with the belief that Christ is our guide, so *we* don't need to offer advice. Christ does the advising.

The committee's function is to create a space where Christ's voice can be heard. The clearness committee listens with open hearts and minds and affirms the person's desire for clearness, facilitating the drawing out of the person's Inner Teacher. Such "space-making" and listening affirms that we are all Spirit led, but that there are times when we need the assistance of others in clarifying our leadings.

Discernment groups have a long ecumenical history of carrying out vital spiritual work. As St. John of the Cross writes:

> Thus God announces that he does not want the soul to believe only by itself the communications it thinks are of divine origin, or for anyone to be assured or confirmed in them without the Church or her ministers. God will not bring clarification and confirmation of the truth to the heart of one who is alone. Such a person would remain weak and cold in regard to truth.

Listening to the Gathered Friends

In addition to encouraging a seeking friend to listen to Christ the Inner Teacher, a clearness committee also encourages the seeker to listen to his or her spiritual friends, not as advice givers, but as Christ pointers. The clearness committee is a sort of Christ the Outer Teacher. This is equally true if the committee's words confirm Christ's or if their questions point out things that had not been considered.

As a friend of mine noted, this last part—a person's willingness to heed the wisdom of others—is crucial to successfully following a leading. She told me of a time when someone requested a clearness committee regarding whether to continue in a responsible position. My friend said the committee couldn't do its work because this person came to the gathering with his mind made up. He would not hear what his spiritual friends were asking, and so he missed the wisdom coming from God through his friends. However, when the person is open to the voice of God through others, the Holy Spirit works to bring unity.

Bathed in Prayer

A clearness committee works best when it submerges itself in prayer, because prayer opens us to God. Prayer leads us into a dialogue of Spirit to spirit. Being in an attitude of prayer gives us a clear channel to God and opens the group's collective spiritual ears to God's voice. As we hear God's voice, we jointly discern the way forward—or see that a stop sign has been placed in our path.

Prayer helps the committee sense God present in their process. Prayer keeps us from merely going through the motions of being a clearness committee, as though there was magic in the process. Prayer leads us to a place as a group of spiritual friends where God's presence with us is felt.

The Joy of the Lord

Just because a clearness committee's attitude needs to be one of prayer, doesn't mean that it is devoid of playfulness. Don't undertake group discernment in grim earnestness. Leadings are ultimately life giving; they lead to the face of a loving God. Joy fills such an encounter. Therefore, joy must be present in any process that leads us to God. We find soul satisfaction in following a will beyond our own. The sacred compass takes us to a place beyond our imagining—into the company of God. Times of joy and laughter are part of such work.

Be Still

Begin and end the committee's time together with being quiet before God. Center your thoughts on God and let go of the myriad thoughts and concerns racing through your head. That letting go is important if you want to be open to the divine word. Too many of your own words and thoughts buzzing around make it easy to miss which way the sacred compass is pointing. Aim for communal stillness and openness to God's word to and through the group. And remember, the goal as a group is to guide—not lead. Let God lead.

Hi, My Name Is...

Next, take a brief time to get to know one another. The more we know one another, the better we understand each other and the various viewpoints that will arise while we do this spiritual work together. That understanding helps us ask deeper clarifying questions and identify themes that bring us together. Personal friendship teaches us to trust the others we're seeking with and think the best of them instead of wondering how they ever came up with such a silly thought. Invite those gathered to share their spiritual stories. One exercise I've used is to ask participants to finish the sentence, "The earliest spiritual experience I can remember is . . . " A question like that helps us get to know each other in an important way—and reminds us why we are gathered—for important soulful work.

Be Quiet

Silence is essential to a clearness committee's success. Silence is especially crucial as people begin speaking to or about the leading. Be slow to respond or answer. An unrushed silence gives words time to season. Silence gives the words the room to settle in to the mind and spirit, so both the mind and spirit will hear them.

Silence also gives the group time to ponder, so keep the following in mind:

- Take a breath.
- Put the thought away.
- Settle your body.
- Calm your mind.
- If a thought persists, give it time to percolate and become full-bodied before sharing.
- Don't just do something—sit there!

Silence lets you listen to God, sift your thoughts, decide whether to speak or not, and pray. And pray. And pray.

Speak Truth and Love

If we pay careful attention, a time to speak will come. Again, focus on asking questions, not making statements. Ask your questions in a tone of love. They can be challenging, but only so much as is needed to help the person fully test his or her leading. You're not asking questions in an attempt to quench the person's leading. You're asking them to open the person up to the Spirit.

Good questions are sensitive, seeking, and practical, such as:

◆ Do you need any special training to be prepared to follow this leading?

◆ How will you cover your expenses on this trip?

You should also ask questions that engage the person's imagination and spirit, such as:

◆ Why do you think God has called you to this work?

◆ How do you see this changing your spiritual life?

◆ Where will following this leading take you?

Take time for silence after asking each question. It's important to give the person a chance to think and weigh responses before speaking. Whatever you do, don't ask questions that have an implied "right" answer. It's fine, though, to hold people accountable for honesty with themselves, their situation, and God.

Listen Deeply

Listen well and carefully. Dare to ask if the voice being heard is the voice of God or the voice of ego. This brings discernment back to the most important question—*to whom am I listening?* With that question in mind and soul, listen for:

- ◆ dissonance or divergence
- ◆ separation between what's being said and what's being sensed
- ◆ thoughts and feelings that seem to be moving toward each other
- ◆ recurring words and phrases, and what that recurrence reveals
- ◆ clues to discernment
- ◆ the tone behind the words
- ◆ joy, nervousness, excitement, or despair

Also listen for:

- ◆ places of unity
- ◆ the sense of the committee
- ◆ agreement
- ◆ disharmony
- ◆ confirmation of the leading
- ◆ deeper questioning

We must look, too, for how the fruits of the spirit—love, joy, peace, longsuffering, gentleness, goodness, faith, meekness, and temperance—are apparent in the words we're hearing from the group and the person examining the leading. If they are present, it is a good sign that the leading comes from God. If they are not . . .

Concluding

Eventually, the time comes when the work is winding down. Before you close your time together, make sure everyone is ready to do so. Remember that the group members were asked to participate because of their spiritual wisdom. If someone says he or she is not ready to close, trust his or her spiritual leading. Time is of the essence—but that essence has to be of spiritual deliberation, not haste. It has to be God's time, not ours.

Ignore any internal human insistence to move things along. That kind of time keeping can stop the group's spiritual sensitivity by calling attention to something external, rather than letting them focus on the eternal internal. Worrying about time can keep the group from arriving at a deep place of spiritual wisdom.

◆

My friend Jane followed her leading to go back into newspaper journalism. Then she had another leading. And another. Sometimes she called me to test those leadings. One time I called her to share leading I had about her. The job she has today came as the result of her sensing, testing, and following her leadings, and as the result of her spiritual friends offering traveler's aid to her.

EIGHT

THE DANCE OF DISCERNMENT
The Gift and Responsibility of the Way

F LYING OUT OF INDIANAPOLIS ONE DAY, the flight path took us almost over my house. Forgetting for a few moments how much I hate flying, I looked out and down. After a few seconds, I picked out our long gravel drive, the field of sprouting wildflowers and prairie grass, the woods, and our house. I watched for the few moments they stayed in sight. Then I sat back in my seat. I smiled inside. I thought how blessed I was. The holy path, even though it has lead through some difficult places, has so far taken me to a place of beauty and blessing. I'm fortunate to be a father, grandfather, husband, boss, writer, occasional tractor driver, and tree and prairie grass farmer.

All of this has been a gift from God. None of it has come through dint of personal achievement. It didn't come as the result of my schooling, talents, or amazing intellect. Certainly all of those things played into how the path opened. Indeed, they were parts of the path—going to a college where I'd meet a wise mentor who continues to influence my spiritual and writing life; being welcomed into a large and loving stepfamily; joining the staff of the Center for Congregations.

Why these blessings have come my way is as mysterious to me as quantum physics. I don't understand either blessings or valence shell electrons. What I do understand is that since God has led me to the places I've been and the blessings I have, I have a responsibility to use them wisely and well and for something more than my own ease or personal enjoyment.

This responsibility is the main reason Nancy and I planted thousands of trees under whose shade we'll never sit and whose fruit we'll likely never enjoy. Other people will—and will be blessed indirectly by our blessing. And the world's air will be cleaner thanks to those trees. We didn't plant the trees because we're particularly good people (well, Nancy is . . .). Rather, we did it because it's part of our responsibility to be good stewards of that with which we've been blessed. As Jesus said, "From everyone to whom much has been given, much will be required; and from the one to whom much has been entrusted, even more will be demanded."

This thought came alive for me one morning when I walked our prairie. Though I couldn't remember who said it, the words, "You never really know your land until you walk it" came to me. Canadian thistles had sprung up in multitudes. I had slung on my backpack sprayer and was killing them so they wouldn't overwhelm the wildflowers and prairie grasses. Though I had driven over the property many times before, during this walk I sensed the subtle risings and fallings in the land that looks flat to the eye or feels flat to the tush on a tractor. The soles of my feet communicated to my soul the infinite variety of topography on our nine-acre prairie—soft ground, hard ground, mats of grass, and thick stems of ironweed. My "eye-view" was lower than usual, too, so I saw the ground and growth differently—rattlesnake master and brown-eyed Susans beginning to bloom, bluestem grass reaching slowly toward the sun. There were rabbits where there'd been no rabbits before, butterflies fluttering by, and red-winged blackbirds calling out, warning me not to come too close to their nests.

All in all, besides increasing my love of the place I call home, my walk that day drove home the responsibility I have to keep the land tended as well as I can so that someday there will be even more rabbits, butterflies, deer, and someday, wild turkey and quail. It reminded me of the joyous, ecstatic creativity of God when this was all called into being by a word. It reminded me that I'm a more attentive person to God around me when I'm walking than I am when I'm mechanized—whether driving across the prairie or speeding through life. Walking fits with the pilgrim life. God has opened the way for me to be a father, grandfather, husband, boss, writer, and tree and prairie grass farmer for a reason. I have a responsibility to live up to the way. "And your ears shall hear a word behind you, saying, 'This is the way, walk in it.'"

Walking the prairie is also a part of the path of God's continuing revelation to me. This is another part of the responsibility of the way—the responsibility of continual learning and deepening. The actual act of walking the prairie is spiritually renewing, but it is also a metaphor for how I should be moving through life—which is with my spiritual feet on the ground feeling the terrain and my spiritual eyes following the path and looking for the signs that will help me navigate successfully. Those signs come in a variety of ways—through people I meet, books that friends think I should read, music I hear, a question I'm asked. All of life, when we live as pilgrims, is a spiritual experience—an opportunity for living deeper into God's grace.

Besides the responsibilities of being a wise steward and lifelong learner, another responsibility is the need to be obedient. I am an unruly spiritual child during the best of times; I'm sure God must frequently slap his head in a Homer Simpson–esque fashion and mutter to the heavenly host, "What is he up to now?" If left to my own way, and the inner laziness and willfulness that I have, my life would truly be a mess. Following the holy path has led me to an understanding that, for me, obedience to God's way brings joy and order. Being a type-A personality, that last part is especially happy news for me. I like order. And while there is a wildness in God's mercy (as we used to mis-sing the old hymn "There's a Wideness in God's Mercy"), my life is more joyful when I don't have to rely on that mercy to save me from the messes that obedience would have kept me out of. Anne Lamott, in her book *Traveling Mercies*, claims the best two prayers she knows are "Help me, help me, help me" and "Thank you, thank you, thank you." Obedience, for me, leads me to a place where I pray the latter more than the former.

Another responsibility of following the path of discernment is that I be true. I need to be faithful to the leadings I've been given, and not just when they are convenient or easy. I hear Jesus saying, "Why do you call me 'Lord, Lord,' and not do what I tell you?"

To follow a leading to help with our congregation's Quaker Day cooking is easy, but other leadings are not. I read the paper one day and saw that the police arrested a pastor friend of mine during a protest for workers' rights. While I didn't have the same leading to do what she did, I wondered in my heart if I could go to jail if I had. Jail would have been really inconvenient for me, both physically (the whole diabetes thing) and career-wise (possibly jeopardizing my organization's standing in the community with those who disagree with the cause). Could I be true to the end—like Tom Fox, or just for an overnight in the county lock-up? Or would I instead convince myself that I must have listened to the wrong voice? I hear Jesus saying, "You are my friends if you do what I command," and hope I'm able to be a true friend. The longer I walk the holy path, the more I want to be that kind of man.

There are other responsibilities that I sense the holy path requires of me—to be more loving (and not just to those I think are deserving of my love), more active physically and spiritually, and more understanding of others' points of view. The way may require these responsibilities, or something completely different from you. The responsibilities take us to the growing edge of this life of faith. They teach us, as they shift and change along with our path, that as pilgrims, we are always in motion. That holy motion keeps us growing. Living into the responsibilities of the holy path helps our lives bear witness to the force of God's love in them. People can see us growing deeper. And even if they can't, we can.

◆

The paths we are led to come from the unfathomable mind and love of God. While our minds cause us to cry out, "Why?" we are rarely offered an explanation. Rather, we hear an invitation—the invitation to join in creation's continuing dance to the Spirit's song. It is the invitation to follow the sacred compass. It is the invitation to "Stand by the roads, and look, and ask for the ancient paths, where the good way is; and walk in it, and find rest for your souls."

HIKING EQUIPMENT
Additional Resources for Following the Sacred Compass

It's essential to take the right gear when you start out on a hike—be it an hour-long walk in the woods or a lifetime trek to God. Below are some things you might find helpful to have in your spiritual backpack.

COMPASS CALIBRATION
Questions for Spiritual Growth

The following questions for spiritual growth are based on the Friends practice of asking "queries." Quakers use queries as individual and corporate questions for gauging their spiritual growth and health. The following questions for spiritual reflection are meant for guided self-examination. They aren't a set of rules. There are no set right answers that apply to everyone. Rather, the answers are right depending on the person asking them—you. Use them by relaxing your body and mind, breathing deeply, and contemplating both the questions and your responses gently, slowly, and soulfully.

Questions for Spiritual Growth for Individuals

Can I separate my feelings and emotions and listen to God?
Do I have faith that God will carry me when I feel too weak to move?

Do I have habits that keep me from following my leading?

Do I trust God to give me the strength I need to follow my leading?

Have I been faithful in following my leading to this point?

How do I experience and care for the discernment I feel within my soul?

How do I experience Christ as my Inner Teacher?

What am I being called to do or to be at this time in my life?

What can I do to help me hear God more clearly?

What do I need—physically, emotionally, spiritually—to follow my leading?

What does the idea of "divine guidance" mean to me?

What feels alive inside of me?

What must I stop doing for me to hear God more clearly?

Questions for Spiritual Growth for Clearness Committees

Does the leading clash in any harmful way with your friend's personal, work, or other commitments?

Does the leading feel God inspired?

Does the leading show evidence of the fruits of the Spirit (love, joy, peace, patience, kindness, goodness, faithfulness, gentleness, and self-control)?

Is the leading consistent with your friend's gifts and life experiences?

Is the leading in harmony with Scripture?

Is there a specific reason that you feel that your friend shouldn't follow his or her leading?

FIRE STARTERS
Prayers for Pilgrims

William McGill, a nineteenth-century Episcopal priest, said, "The value of consistent prayer is not that He will hear us, but that we will hear Him." The following prayers have that goal in mind—that God's voice might be heard as we follow our sacred compass:

◆

Eternal God, let thy spirit inspire and guide us. Thy will be done. Give us the strength to fulfill our task without selfishness, slothfulness, or cowardice. . . . Eternal God, we will listen to thy call and obey it in order that we may hear it ever more clearly. Give us the honesty to examine our own acts and thoughts as scrupulously and severely as those of other people. . . . Give us the quiet courage needed in all circumstances and natural to whoever has consecrated his life to thee. . . . Do not let any defeat, any fall . . . separate us from thee; in the midst of all our weakness let thy love take hold of us and little by little lift us up to thee.

◆

Grant me, O Lord, to know what I ought to know . . . to discern with a true judgment between things visible and spiritual, and above all things, always to inquire what is the good pleasure of your will.

◆

Great God of Love, who calls us with a winsomeness we cannot resist and binds us to yourself and each other with cords of beauty, truth, joy, and sorrow, we come to worship you today. We come asking for daily bread, but not for wealth, lest we forget the poor; asking for strength, but not for power, lest we despise the meek; asking for faith, but not for certainty, lest we disdain those seeking thee in ways different than our own; asking for peace of mind, but not for idle hours, lest we fail to hearken to your call to service. Amen.

◆

O Lord, I do not know what to ask you. You alone know my real needs, and you love me more than I even know how to love. Enable me to discern my true needs which are hidden from me. I ask for neither cross nor consolation; I wait in patience for you. My heart is open to you. For your great mercy's sake come to me and help me. Put your mark on me and heal me, cast me down and raise me up. Silently I adore your holy will and your inscrutable ways. I offer myself in sacrifice to you and put all my trust in you. I desire only to do your will. Teach me how to pray and pray in me, yourself.

◆

I am no longer my own, but yours. Put me to what you will, rank me with whom you will. Put me to doing, put me to suffering. Let me be employed by you or laid aside for you, exalted for you or brought low for you. Let me be full, let me be empty. Let me have all things, let me have nothing. I freely and heartily yield all things to your pleasure and disposal. And now, O glorious and blessed God, Father, Son, and Holy Spirit, you are mine, and I am yours. So be it. And the covenant I have made on earth, let it be ratified in heaven. Amen.

◆

God our Creator, you have plans for me. You present me with the gift of a hope-filled future. Grant me wisdom from your Spirit so that I see in the life I live and the gifts you've given me the plans you have for me. Help me to seek you with all my heart, and the will to follow where you lead. Amen.

◆

God of my life, I give you thanks and praise that I have life, and that my life is filled with touches of your love. You have given me a heart that wants to be happy, and You have placed in me a desire to make a difference. Quiet the fears and distractions of my heart long enough for me to listen to the movement of Your Spirit, to hear your gentle invitation. Reveal to me the choices that will make me happy. Help me to discover my identity. Let me understand how best to use the gifts You have so lovingly lavished upon me in preparation for our journey together. And give me the courage to choose You as You have chosen me. Lord, let me know myself and let me know You. In this is my happiness. Amen.

◆

God, I know you love me and have wonderful plans for my life. But sometimes thoughts for the future overwhelm me. Life feels so immense. Teach me how to walk your path one day at a time and leave tomorrow for its time. Grant me courage as I seek your ways. Help me to listen to others—and myself. Take me to places where I can follow you as I should and love you as I wish. Help me to see and appreciate and use the gifts and life you've given me. Amen.

◆

Most High, glorious God, enlighten the darkness of my heart, and give me right faith, certain hope, and perfect charity, wisdom, and understanding, Lord, that I may carry out your holy and true command. Amen.

FIRST AID SUPPLIES
Books and Web Resources for the Journey

In addition to the books mentioned throughout this book and in the chapter endnotes, below are some resources that are especially worth noting for their valuable insight to the art and nature of discernment.

Books

Boers, Arthur Paul. *The Way Is Made by Walking: A Pilgrimage Along the Camino de Santiago*. Downers Grove, IL: InterVarsity Press, 2007. The story of a Mennonite who goes on a mostly Catholic pilgrimage. Challenging, thoughtful, and spiritually enriching, Boers's book unlocks the value of pilgrimage for himself and his readers.

Caliguire, Mindy. *Spiritual Friendship*. Downers Grove, IL: InterVarsity Press, 2007. A brief, practical, and informative guide for learning about, overcoming the barriers to, and ultimately forging spiritual friendships.

Farrington, Debra K. *Hearing with the Heart: A Gentle Guide for Discerning God's Will for Your Life*. San Francisco: Jossey-Bass, 2003. A tender, wise book that teaches us how to listen with our hearts and not just our heads. I rarely have a copy of this on my shelf because I keep giving it away.

Foster, Richard J., and Emilie Griffin, eds. *Spiritual Classics: Selected Readings for Individuals and Groups on the Twelve Spiritual Disciplines*. San Francisco: HarperSanFrancisco,

2000. A wonderful guide to twelve classic spiritual disciplines (meditation, prayer, fasting, study, simplicity, solitude, submission, service, confession, worship, guidance, and celebration) as experienced by the likes of St. Augustine, Evelyn Underhill, Anne Morrow Lindbergh, and Frederick Buechner. This is a good resource for both personal and group study.

Loring, Patricia. *Listening Spirituality.* Vol. 1, *Personal Spiritual Practices Among Friends.* Washington Grove, MD: Openings Press, 1997. Loring's book is one to live with and work through. Her writing is deep and insightful, and her book offers sound advice and helpful exercises and resources for experiencing spiritual practices as tools for discernment.

Padrick, Stacey. *Living With Mystery: Finding God in the Midst of Unanswered Questions.* Minneapolis: Bethany House, 2003. Drawing on a rich variety of sources, Padrick takes the reader to a safe, hospitable place where the deep questions of disappointment and faith are examined honestly and fearlessly. Ultimately, Stacey's frank vulnerability and words of encouragement inspire readers to take comfort in life's journey with all its twists and turns, confident in the deep love and graciousness of God.

Palmer, Parker J. *Let Your Life Speak: Listening for the Voice of Vocation.* San Francisco: Jossey-Bass, 2000. A classic about discerning life's and God's best choices, particularly as they concern vocation.

Smith, Carol Ann, and Eugene F. Merz. *Finding God in Each Moment: The Practice of Discernment in Everyday Life*. Notre Dame, IN: Ave Maria Press, 2006. Using the writings of St. Ignatius, coupled with Scripture and documents from Vatican II, *Finding God in Each Moment* is filled with daily exercises for doing just that.

Discernment Online

For online information and practical help about discernment, visit Practicing Our Faith (http://www.practicingourfaith.org). Sponsored by the Valparaiso Project on the Education and Formation of People in Faith, this project developed resources to help live Christian faith with vitality and integrity in changing times. Each practice offers sections on ways to implement the practice, what others are doing in that practice, and additional resources (sermons, study guides, and so forth).

I learned about the Irish Jesuit site Sacred Space (http://www.sacredspace.ie) while writing this book. A friend of mine told me that he visits it daily. The site's mission is to help you "make a 'Sacred Space' in your day, and spend ten minutes, praying here and now, as you sit at your computer." It uses Scripture and on-screen guides to practice spiritual formation in the midst of daily life.

ACKNOWLEDGMENTS

As Aelred of Rievaulx wrote, "But only those do we call friends to whom we can fearlessly entrust our hearts and all our secrets." Those kinds of friends assisted me with this book. I entrusted them with my heart and secrets as revealed in this writing, and they guided me in shaping it into something I hope you'll find encouraging and helpful.

I am grateful to Tim Shapiro and Susan Weber, coworkers and people of deep spiritual insight, for offering encouragement and wise advice.

I am also grateful to Don Ottenhoff of the Ecumenical Institute at St. John's University and Seminary and Cynthia Malone of the College of St. Benedict. I spent a week with them at a "writer's asylum" in Collegeville, Minnesota, as the seed of this book first came to life. Don, Cynthia, and the other participating writers lent critical eyes and kind hearts to the initial thoughts and stories.

Likewise, as the book progressed, many friends participated in conversations, surveys, e-mail discussions, and blog responses to questions I had about their spiritual practices and discernment experiences. To them all, whether their stories appear in this book or not, I offer my deepest thanks. I'm especially grateful to Bob Gosney who let me share his story—and reconnect after many years of dormant friendship.

Lil Copan, my editor at Paraclete Press, pushes me to write poetic prose. She helps me see myself as a better writer than I am—and in doing so makes me and my writing better. Thanks, too, to the many other fine folks at Paraclete who believed in this project and worked to bring it to life.

Finally, there's Nancy. From proofreading manuscripts to sharing her spiritual stories and wonderment, she is a helpmeet in every way. Asking her to marry me was the best bit of discernment I've ever practiced—though I'm not sure she could say the reverse is true! Thanks, Nancy—and thanks to everyone else, too, for tending to my heart and secrets with so much care.

PERMISSIONS

POETRY

NOTES

INTRODUCTION

xiii   *there are different wells*   Daniel Ledinsky, trans., *The Gift: Poems by Hafiz the Great Sufi Master* (New York: Penguin, 1999).

CHAPTER ONE

3   *the word of the Lord was precious*   1 Samuel 3:1 (KJV).
    And [Jesus] withdrew from them   Luke 22:41–42 (RSV).

4   *train yourself to be godly*   1 Timothy 4:7–8 (NIV).

5   *healthy, balanced church*   40 Days of Purpose, http://www.purposedriven.com/en-US/40DayCampaigns/40DaysOfPurpose/40DOPHOME.htm.

6   *If you love me*   John 14:15–17 (RSV).

7   *Go out and stand on the mountain*   1 Kings 19:11–13.

10   *A Prayer for Owen Meany*   John Irving (New York: Modern Library, 2002).

12   *Know what it is to walk*   A.W. Ward et al., eds., *The Cambridge History of English and American Literature: An Encyclopedia in Eighteen Volumes* (New York: G.P. Putnam's Sons, 1907–21). Available at http://www.bartleby.com/218/0407.html. Modernization mine.

14   *Indeed, every true word*   "Conversion" in *A Spiritual Journey,* cited in *God in All Worlds: An Anthology of Contemporary Spiritual Writing,* ed. Lucinda Vardey (New York: Vintage Books, 1995), 12.

15   *I lift up my eyes to the hills*   Psalm 121 (RSV).

17   *My Lord God, I have no idea*   Thomas Merton, "Prayer of Trust and Confidence" in *Thoughts in Solitude* (New York: Farrar, Straus and Giroux, 1999), 79.

19 *a monument only says*   Quoted in Eugene Peterson, *A Long Obedience in the Same Direction: Discipleship in an Instant Society* (Illinois: InterVarsity Press, 1980), 17.

CHAPTER TWO

24 *love what it loves*   Mary Oliver, "Wild Geese" in *Dream Work* (Boston: Atlantic Monthly Press, 1986).
In trying to answer the question   Dan Wakefield, *Spiritually Incorrect: Finding God in All the Wrong Places* (Woodstock, VT: Skylight Paths Publishing, 2004), 18.

27 *Our lives speak through our stories*   Another way of letting your life speak to you through your story is by accepting the invitation of the radio show *This I Believe* to write an essay on what matters most to you. This popular National Public Radio program is based on a program of the same name that debuted in the 1950s. Thousands of people from around the world have written and submitted their own short (350–500 words) statements of personal belief. The show's guidelines for writing such an essay are helpful—even if you never submit your essay. You can view them at http://thisibelieve.org/essaywritingtips.html.

Our reading club did this as part of our discussion of the essays compiled into the book *This I Believe*. Everybody in the group who tried writing an essay talked about how easy and hard it was. But they mostly noted how revealing it was—how writing about what they believed helped illuminate for themselves what they believed. The act of putting faith into words helped them see the divine at work in their lives.

30 *O Lord, thou art our Father*   Isaiah 64:8 (KJV).
Does the clay say to him   Isaiah 45:9 (RSV).

33 *Jacob dreamt of a stairway to heaven*   Genesis 28:10–22.
King Nebuchadnezzar had a dream   Daniel 4.
Pharaoh's dreams sprung Joseph from jail   Genesis 41.

the Magi were warned in a dream   Matthew 2:12.

35 *There are many voices in the night*   Walter Brueggermann, "The Power of Dreams in the Bible," *The Christian Century*, June 28, 2005, 28–31.

36 *All [of us] have access to God*   Martin Buber, *The Way of Man: According to the Teachings of Hasidism,* Pendle Hill Pamphlets 106 (Wallingford, PA: Pendle Hill Pamphlets, 1960), 13.
    Perfection consists in being   www.catholicforum.com/saints/saintt02.html.

38 *Lose not thy confidence*   Thomas à Kempis, *The Imitation of Christ: The Inspirational Teachings of Thomas à Kempis* (New York: Sterling Publishing, 2006), 36.

41 *Debra Farrington says*   Debra K. Farrington, *Hearing with the Heart: A Gentle Guide to Discerning God's Will for Your Life* (San Francisco: Jossey-Bass, 2003).

43 *My name is Legion*   Mark 5:9–10 (NIV).

44 *asked God if it was okay*   Kaylin Haught, from Kowit, *The Palm of Your Hand,* 6.

46 *is to me a source of love*   Anna Bidder, quoted in *Quaker Faith and Practice: Second Edition* (London: The Yearly Meeting of the Religious Society of Friends [Quakers] in Britain), 21.08.

CHAPTER THREE

47 *Take heed of the promptings*   Quaker Faith and Practice: Second Edition, 26.01.

48 *For I was hungry*   Matthew 25:35.

49 *For where two or three*   Matthew 18:20 (RSV).
    God be in my head   Sarum Primer, ca. 1514, in *The Book of Common Worship* (Louisville, KY: Westminster John Knox Press, 1993).

51 *Speak, Lord, for your servant hears*   Christina Rossetti quoted at http://www.thisischurch.com/partnershipnews/ partnershipnews29may2005.pdf.

52 *God knew*   John Muhanji quoted at http://www.fum.org/QL/ issues/0605/news.htm.

53 *Many other Friends have written wisely*   Quakers Paul Lacey, Jane Orion Smith, Hugh Barbour, Patricia Loring, and Jerrilyn Prior have offered some especially helpful tips in their writings, many of which are available online.

54 *God is in all beauty*   Caroline C. Graveson quoted in *Quaker Faith and Practice: Second Edition,* 21.28.

57 *Be patient and still*   Hugh Barbour, Five Tests for Discerning a True Leading, at http://www.tractassociation.org/ FiveTestsForDiscerningATrueLeading.html.
The vocation for you   http://www.pbs.org/wnet/ religionandethics/week936/profile.html.

58 *When Christ calls a man*   Dietrich Bonhoeffer, *The Cost of Discipleship* (New York: Macmillan Publishing Company, 1963), 7.

59 *The central issue is always*   Taken from the 2001 minutes of the Iowa Yearly Meeting of Friends (Conservative), http:// quakernet.org.

60 *Woe is me!*   Isaiah 6:5,8 (RSV).
Oh, my LORD, I am not eloquent   Exodus 4:10–12 (RSV).

61 *I'm glad I was here*   George Fox, *The Journal of George Fox,* ed. John L. Nickalls (London: Religious Society of Friends, 1975), 752.

62 *the fruits of spirit*   Galatians 5:22–23.

64 *I am the LORD your God*   Isaiah 48:17.

CHAPTER FOUR

71 *God has a plan*   Robert Hellenga, *Philosophy Made Simple* (New York: Back Bay Books, 2007), 191.

72 *Ask, and it will be given you* Luke 11:9 (RSV).

76 *Sifting apart* http://godsfriends.org/Vol14/No2/sifting-sorting. html.

80 *Lectio divina invites us to study* For a good introduction to *lectio divina,* my favorite website is Fr. Luke Dysinger, "Accepting the Embrace of God: The Ancient Art of *Lectio Divina*," at http:// www.valyermo.com/ld-art.html.

82 *Despite its similarity to the word* examination Debra K. Farrington, *Hearing with the Heart,* 66.

89 *Margaret Guenther says the characteristics* David G. Benner, *Sacred Companions* (Downers Grove, IL: InterVarsity Press, 2002), 46.

94 *The art of living must be studied* Horace B. Pointing, quoted in *Quaker Faith and Practice: Second Edition,* 21.21.

CHAPTER FIVE

99 *Are you the only visitor* Luke 24:18 (RSV).

101 *usually summed up* Arthur Paul Boers, *The Way Is Made by Walking: A Pilgrimage Along the Camino de Santiago* (Downers Grove, IL: InterVarsity Press, 2007), 22.
In the tradition of pilgrimage Parker Palmer, *Let Your Life Speak: Listening of the Voice of Vocation* (San Francisco: Jossey-Bass, 2000), 18.

102 *We know that all things* Romans 8:28 (WORLD ENGLISH ONLINE BIBLE http://online-bible-study.net/parallel-bible/wld-dby/ Romans/8/).

103 *The silence and the emptiness* David Van Biema, "Mother Teresa's Crisis of Faith," *Time,* Thursday, August 23, 2007. Available at http://www.time.com/time/world/article/0,8599,1655415,00. html.

104 *Now that Mother Theresa* Catharine Phillips, "Mother Theresa." Unpublished poem used with permission.

107 *Oh God, take me* Etty Hillesum quoted at http://www.
magazine.feminenza.org/issue001/etty_hillesum.htm.
Sometimes when I stand Philip Yancey, *Prayer: Does It Make Any
Difference?* (Grand Rapids: Zondervan, 2006), 51.

110 *There's a reason for living* Noel Stookey, "John Henry
Bosworth," *Songbirds of Paradise,* copyright 1971. From the
album *Paul and . . .,* Warner Brothers, 1971.

112 *the lost coin* Luke 15:8–9.

113 *Faith is not synonymous* Doris Bett quoted at http://dnn.
northminster-indy.org/LinkClick.aspx?link=Sermons%2FMarc
h272005Sermon.doc&tabid=155&mid=542.
Almighty and most merciful *The Book of Common Prayer* (1928).
Available at http://justus.anglican.org/resources/bcp/1928/EP.htm.

114 *Search me, O God* Psalm 139:23–24 (KJV).
There can be times Patricia Loring, *Spiritual Discernment: The
Context and Goal of Clearness Committees,* Pendle Hill Pamphlets
305 (Wallingford, PA: Pendle Hill Pamphlets, 1992), 12.

115 *There is as much guidance* Parker Palmer, *Let Your Life Speak,* 54.

122 *You thick one* C.S. Lewis, *Out of the Silent Planet* (New York:
Quality Paperback Bookclub, 1997), 133.
Whatever we may have to go through Romans 8:18–19 (PHILLIPS).
in the end the whole Romans 8:21 (PHILLIPS).

123 *it is plain to anyone* Romans 18:22–28 (PHILLIPS).
O LORD, you have searched me Psalm 139:1–6 (PHILLIPS).

124 *The time of fear is over* G. Peter Fleck, *Come as You Are:
Reflections on the Revelations of Everyday Life* (Boston, Beacon
Press, 1993), 46.

125 *the kind of mind* Flannery O'Connor, *Mystery and Manners:
Occasional Prose* (New York: Farrar, Straus & Giroux, 1969).
Where can I go Psalm 139:7.

126 *It's like so many other things in life* Thomas R. Smith, "Trust,"
in *Waking before Dawn* (Northfield, MN: Red Dragonfly Press,
2007).

CHAPTER SIX

127 *Does that mean I walk*   Tom Fox, Fight or Flight, http://waitinginthelight.blogspot.com/2004/10/fight-or-flight.html.

128 *To have experienced*   Martin Bell, *The Way of the Wolf* (New York: The Seabury Press, 1970), 43.

129 *Jesus called Peter out of the boat*   See Matthew 14:22–31.
    O God, by whom the meek   Geoffrey Rowell, Kenneth Stevenson, and Rowan Williams, *Love's Redeeming Work: The Anglican Quest for Holiness* (Oxford: Oxford University Press, 2003), 454.

130 *Isolation of spirit*   Edward Milligan quoted in *Quaker Faith and Practice: Second Edition,* 21.20.

132 *My soul magnifies the Lord*   Luke 1:46–55 (RSV).

134 *Although I have often*   Teresa of Avila, http://www.viarosa.com/VR/StTeresa/Avila.html

135 *And the* LORD *God formed*   Genesis 2:7–8 (KJV).

136 *And out of the ground*   Genesis 2:9 (KJV).

137 *We must learn*   Gordon Matthews quoted in *Quaker Faith and Practice: Second Edition,* 29.01.

141 *Let me ask you something*   *Evan Almighty,* screenplay by Steve Oedekerk, © 2007 by Universal Studios.

142 *How do I stay*   Tom Fox, The Middle of Nowhere, http://waitinginthelight.blogspot.com/2005_04_01_archive.html.

144 *Trouble of soul*   Edward Grubb quoted in *Quaker Faith and Practice: Second Edition,* 21.12.
    Be patterns   George Fox quoted at Waiting in the Light, http://waitinginthelight.blogspot.com.

145 *that things that happen*   Dale Brown, *The Book of Buechner: A Journey Through His Writings* (Louisville: Westminster John Knox, 2006), 8.

CHAPTER SEVEN

147 *But it doesn't matter*   J.I. Packer, *Knowing God* (Downers Grove, IL: InterVarsity Press, 1993), 20.

148 *Do not neglect*   1 Timothy 4:14 (HCSB).
Here we are   Spiritual Friendship by Saint Aelred, ed. Mary Eugenia Laker (Collegeville, MN: Cistercian Publications, 1974), 51.

151 *A couple of summers ago*   Harold Kushner, interview by Hugh Hewitt, *Searching for God in America*, PBS, 1997.

152 *Lord Jesus, merciful and patient*   Christina Rossetti, quoted by Michael Counsell in *2000 Years of Prayer* (New York: Morehouse Publishing, 1999), 377.

154 *And all such as behold*   George Fox quoted in *Quaker Faith and Practice: Second Edition*, 12.17.

155 *I recall with sadness*   George Gorman quoted in *Quaker Faith and Practice: Second Edition*, 22.08.

157 *Thus God announces*   Kieran Kavanaugh, *John of the Cross: Selected Writings* (Mahwah, NJ: Paulist Press, 1987), 31.

CHAPTER EIGHT

165 *From everyone to whom*   Luke 12:48.

166 *And your ears shall hear*   Isaiah 30:21 (RSV).

168 *Help me*   Anne Lamott, *Traveling Mercies: Some Thoughts on Faith* (New York: Pantheon Books, 1999).
Why do you call me   Luke 6:46 (ESV).
You are my friends   John 15:14 (NIV).

169 *Stand by the roads*   Jeremiah 6:16 (RSV).

HIKING EQUIPMENT

172 *The value of constant prayer*   John Cook, *The Book of Positive Quotations* (Minneapolis: Fairview Press, 2007), 77.

Eternal God, let thy spirit   A prayer written in prison in 1945 by Pierre Ceresole, a Swiss Quaker and peace activist. He died at age forty-eight, shortly after writing this prayer. Quoted in *Christian Faith and Practice in the Experience of the Society of Friends* (London: London Yearly Meeting of the Religious Society of Friends, 1960), 103.

Grant me, O Lord   Thomas à Kempis, *The Imitation of Christ*, 233.

173 *Great God of Love*   A prayer by Brent Bill based in part on a prayer by Inazo Nitobe, a samurai who became a Quaker in the nineteenth century, quoted in *Christian Faith and Practice in the Experience of the Society of Friends,* 1960, p. 90.

O Lord, I do not know   A prayer by Vasily Drosdov Philaret. Philaret, who died in 1867, was a Russian prelate and preacher who wrote a standard catechism of the Russian Orthodox Church. www.orthodox.net/trebnic/of-philaret-of-moscow.html.

I am no longer my own   A prayer by John Wesley known as the Covenant Prayer. Available at http://www.gbod.org/smallgroup/cdjournal.pdf.

174 *God our Creator*   Adapted from a prayer by the Conference of Diocesan Vocations Directors at http://www.vocations.ie/prayer.html#one.

God of my life   "An Augustinian Prayer for Vocational Discernment," from the Augustinians of the Midwest. Available at http://www.midwestaugustinians.org/vocatprayer.html.

175 *God, I know you love me*   Based on a prayer from "Vocation Prayers" at http://www.catholicozvocations.org.au/vocation_prayers/index.html.

Most High, glorious God   St. Francis, "Prayer of Discernment Said Before the Crucifix,"www.franciscanstor.org/prayers.htm

ABOUT THE AUTHOR

In addition to his ministry of writing, J. Brent Bill also enjoys a ministry of leading workshops and speaking. Some of his most popular workshops are:

- ◆ The Sacred Compass: Spiritual Practices for Discernment
- ◆ Being Quiet: The Practice of Holy Silence
- ◆ Sensual Spirituality: Encountering God through the Five Senses
- ◆ Writing from the Heart: Telling Your Soul's Stories

If you would like more information about Brent's writing, or his spirituality workshops and retreats, or would like to contact him about other speaking engagements, you can reach him through his website at www.brentbill.com or via e-mail at brentbil@sbcglobal.net. You can read new material by Brent at holyordinary.blogspot.com, where you can also sign up for an e-newsletter.

ABOUT PARACLETE PRESS

WHO WE ARE

Paraclete Press is an ecumenical publisher of books and recordings on Christian spirituality. Our publishing represents a full expression of Christian belief and practice—from Catholic to Evangelical, from Protestant to Orthodox.

Paraclete Press is the publishing arm of the Community of Jesus, an ecumenical monastic community in the Benedictine tradition. As such, we are uniquely positioned in the marketplace without connection to a large corporation and with informal relationships to many branches and denominations of faith.

We like it best when people buy our books from booksellers, our partners in successfully reaching as wide an audience as possible.

WHAT WE ARE DOING

Books

Paraclete Press publishes books that show the richness and depth of what it means to be Christian. Although Benedictine spirituality is at the heart of all that we do, we publish books that reflect the Christian experience across many cultures, time periods, and houses of worship.

We publish books that nourish the vibrant life of the church and its people—books about spiritual practice, formation, history, ideas, and customs.

We have several different series of books within Paraclete Press, including the best-selling Living Library series of modernized classic texts; A Voice from the Monastery—giving voice to men and women monastics about what it means to live a spiritual life today; award-winning literary faith fiction; and books that explore Judaism and Islam and discover how these faiths inform Christian thought and practice.

Recordings

From Gregorian chant to contemporary American choral works, our music recordings celebrate the richness of sacred choral music through the centuries. Paraclete is proud to distribute the recordings of the internationally acclaimed choir Gloriæ Dei Cantores, who have been praised for their "rapt and fathomless spiritual intensity" by *American Record Guide,* and the Gloriæ Dei Cantores Schola, which specializes in the study and performance of Gregorian chant. Paraclete is also the exclusive North American distributor of the recordings of the Monastic Choir of St. Peter's Abbey in Solesmes, France, long considered to be a leading authority on Gregorian chant performance.

Learn more about us at our Web site:
www.paracletepress.com,
or call us toll-free at
1-800-451-5006.